Quarantining
HATE

Quarantining Hate

Kerrie Taber

Red Engine Press

Fort Smith, Arkansas

Edited by Sandra Miller Linhart

Cover Art by Jay Fox & Kerrie Taber

Cover Design by Joyce Faulkner

Library of Congress Control Number: 2023946913

ISBN: 979-8-9879576-7-7 (softcover)

RED ENGINE
PRESS

Introduction

I had a friend ask me why I was writing this book and what I wanted to get out of writing it. Most people who find skeletons in their family history try to bury them in the dark part of the family closet. If someone found out they had someone in their family who was associated with thousands of deaths, they would pulverize the skeleton and then bury it in the middle of the desert. Why would anyone want to take that information and publish it?

As a professor at a university, I am required to publish in order to get promoted. The need to publish for promotion is not what made me write the book, but it was a bonus. I could focus on publishing in journals in my discipline, but I felt the need to write on the topic of hate. I had used my personal story in discussions with friends and in my classes when we discussed hate. Often, it was because hate never goes away. Going as far as to write a book, however, did not become an idea until recently.

Throughout history there have been peaks and valleys of hate. The United States is reportedly going through a time of increased hate. From 2008 to 2015, reported hate crimes were decreasing in the United States. Then in 2015, the number of reported hate crimes increased. It is not hard to equate the change to a future political leader who openly made fun of people with disabilities, was heard on tape degrading and treating women like objects and reveled in fueling discord.

After becoming elected, he increased division between people by banning travel from Muslim countries and declaring immigrants who crossed the southern border rapists and murderers.

As hate crimes increased and hate groups grew more vocal about their activities and views, the top political leadership remained silent—nothing was said to condemn or rebuke the hate crimes. Our elected officials' silence tacitly condoned their actions, and, during a debate, a white supremacist's group was told to, "Stand down, and stand by."

Years of witnessing blatant hate *not* being condemned, in many ways had me considering doing something beyond teaching a diversity class and responding to friends' social media posts.

Then January 6, 2021 happened—the storming of the Capitol. Like many people, I watched as it unfolded 'live' on the television news. I watched in disbelief. I was appalled when images of a man wearing a Camp Auschwitz shirt and another carrying the Confederate battle flag through the Capitol appeared on my television screen.

Later, I heard interviews with police officers who reported being called racial slurs by rioters as the police were beaten and sprayed with pepper and bear sprays. The incident felt like a culmination of the four-and-a-half years of fueled hate. Watching hate in action and hearing riot witnesses report endured abuse, my desire to react grew. That day's event was the final push that propelled me from thinking to writing a book about my family's history. My story will hopefully give hope that open and thriving hatred can be stopped.

While working on this book, additional events occurred that exemplified the analogy of hate that I sought to incentivize me to finish my story. One of the events was the killing of eight people in Atlanta, six of whom were women of Asian descent.

There had been a rise of violence against people of Asian descent since the start of the COVID-19 pandemic. Before the killings in Atlanta, a ninety-four-year-old man died from injuries he sustained after being assaulted. Others had been attacked for seemingly nothing more than their Asian origin.

Inciteful words from the leader of our country—a land made from immigrants and referred to as a melting pot—fed the hatred. The pandemic turned lives upside down, and rather than dealing with their own personal demons, some sought a scapegoat. Hearing the Coronavirus being called "China" flu, "Kung Fu" flu, and other derogatory terms by political leaders may have emboldened a few American citizens to ostracize and abuse people of Asian descent.

When I started this book, I referred to 'hate' dying or trying to kill 'hate'. That felt insincere as much of my book reported the deaths of so many innocent people. I felt the book already spoke of too much death, but I couldn't find a better way to express my sentiments.

Then, in March 2021, Julian Edelman, a former NFL receiver, published an open letter to Meyers Leonard, an NBA player, after

Leonard was heard using an antisemitic slur while streaming himself play an online game. In the letter, Edelman offered to have Leonard over for Shabbat dinner—a special Jewish Friday meal.

In the letter, Edelman stated, "Hate is a virus. Even accidentally, it can spread rapidly."

When I read his words, I felt the missing piece I searched for fall into place. With the COVID-19 pandemic and the idea that if a person allows hate to be openly spouted without repercussion, referring to 'hate' as a virus fits better.

I don't know what, if any, impact this book will have on people and their propensity to hate. I hope my story will give optimism that something can be done about intolerant hatred. That maybe we can lessen the intensity of hatred and fear with which some people live. That maybe it will support people to encourage those who display that hatred into a quarantine away from society, so that maybe the virus of hate can be stopped.

Table of Contents

Table of Contents

Chapter 1 ~ Hate

No one is born hating another person because of the colour of their skin, or his background, or his religion. People must learn to hate, and if they can learn to hate, they can be taught to love, for love comes more naturally to the human heart than its opposite. —Nelson Mandela

When I was living in the college dorms and a student became ill, the roommate moved out and the sick person remained quarantined. In the dorm's close living quarters, a virus could easily spread. It took a concerted effort of the dorm residents to do whatever they could to stop that spread. Over the past few years, we've witnessed similar actions on a much larger scale to stop the spread of Covid. To slow down the virus' spread, changes were made to limit people's interactions. As much as possible, society quarantined. Schools went virtual, restaurants closed their indoor dining rooms, and non-essential employees worked from their homes.

Hate acts much like a virus in that when society ignores its toxicity, hate group and crime reports rise. Unlike a virus, the person infected by hate is least harmed. Those who are the focus of the hate suffer. The feelings associated with hatred can be the cause of so much pain, suffering, and death when not held in check. 'Hate' is a term often used, but it can be difficult to define. Remper, Burris, and Fathi, in their article about hate, provided the following definition:

"Although it is neither obscene nor profane, 'hate' is arguably one of the most reactive words in the English language. As a phenomenon, hate, is a potent, destructive force that has been implicated in accounts of political oppression, suicide bombings, gang conflicts, and partner abuse, to name a few."

While defining hatred is not easy, determining from where the feeling comes poses additional challenges. People who study hate have not come up with a consensus of its origin. Researchers categorize hate as a variant or subtype of anger—a composite of anger and fear, a composite of anger, disgust, and contempt, and as fear but not anger, disgust, contempt, or envy. Hate can take on a life of its own by spreading throughout a society until it causes harm. The one thing that can be agreed upon is hate is a negative feeling.

Other feelings sometimes categorized as negative include annoyance, melancholy, and sadness. There is something about hate, however, that spreads throughout a society and harms others through hateful actions.

Studies on how people perceive hate and what actions that hate compels them to want to do have been done in Israel. In one study, a quarter of the respondents defined hate as the "wish to experience ill-will, suffering, or death" in the focus of their hate. A third of the participants defined it as an extreme dislike. In another study, the participants saw the hated group as separate and distinct, inferior, and evil. The majority, eighty-three percent wanted to see violent action against the hated group, and fifty percent wanted to see them killed.

While a person may have different negative feelings toward a targeted group, hate seems to be the catalyst for the desire to harm or kill. In a follow-up inquiry to the Israel studies, the participants specified different actions toward a targeted group based on the feelings they felt about that group. If they indicated feeling fear, they identified the action of avoiding the group but had no desire to cause them harm. If they expressed anger toward the group, they wished to educate and change the targeted group. The individuals who disclosed feeling hatred toward a targeted group, professed they wanted to destroy, remove, do evil to, and they supported political and social exclusion of that group. From the Israel study, one can conclude hate motivates people to want to do harm.

Throughout history, hate leading to violence tends to rise from fear and fearmongering. The increase of hate groups is reportedly exacerbated by fear of losing "favored" racial statuses or when a recession hits. The racially bated factions often use others as scapegoats for fear of losing their jobs or status. Organizers of hate groups use those fears to recruit followers and build hate toward others, racially dividing the nation.

With the rise of hate crimes in rural Oregon, preliminary research indicated an increase in hate-group membership after minorities enrolled in a previously all-white school created a fear of losing "favored" race status. The members of the hate group felt interracial mixing in schools led to "hybrid" children due to dilution of "pure" white strength. Such "mixing" in other locations has also led to an increase in hate-group membership. The increased hate crimes trend seems to be tied to a drive for diversity through societal acceptance. As one extremist was quoted as saying, *"Diversity is a code word for white genocide."*

The quote indicates a fear of losing their perceived societal status due to the world's move toward diversity.

For some who fear losing their positions, these groups may give them a sense of belonging, security, and empowerment. Groups can give a person peer validation for similar views, a way to vent frustrations to others who empathize, and can also be a way to address boredom. Humans tend to form groups with other like-minded people. Doing so creates a sense of security that stems from connecting with others. In some cases, that sense of belonging comes from other people who share the same feelings toward another group of people.

Fear that leads to hate-induced violence does not fully explain mass genocide of Armenians by the Turks, Jews by the Nazis, and hate-lynching which predominantly occurred in the southern United States. There is little difference between a hate group inflicting violence upon a targeted group and the societal acceptance and participation in the genocide of a targeted group. Additional elements are needed for hate to rise to an epidemically viral level within the occurring society.

We do not start life recognizing differences between ourselves and others. Our differences are learned from others—family and community. People have the propensity to learn hate, and it quickly spreads throughout communities. Hate groups form as stirring discontent under society's surface. If hatred makes sense to someone at first, that same person may not notice when hatred no longer makes sense. The disconnect allows hatred to infect more people and to increase in size. As hatred resonates with society, extremism grows. This especially can be witnessed within societies who've shown a history of maltreatment.

The lessons in differences hateful people spout often come in the form of devaluing others. They believe someone who is different does not uphold the same values, and therefore should be either ignored, dehumanized, or destroyed. Hate acts much like a virus in that way, as it is often spread from one person to another who is not immune to the message of hating those who are different.

A rescuer of Jewish prisoners after WWII explained the danger of dehumanizing others, *"We have to watch for the old 'Yellow Gooks' mentality. It is much easier to shoot at or burn the 'Yellow Gooks' than to shoot and burn some other farm boy just like yourself."*

In most cases of hate-related violence, the perpetrator of the hate crime saw the victim as sub-human—one who was not due respect.

Societal support—from the public to law enforcement, to elected officials—gives hate the environment it requires to spread and grow to the level where genocide, accepted violence, and murder occurs. In their article on hate, Perry and Scrivens explained how hate can only grow in environments that enable it. They claimed, *"Hate does not emerge in a vacuum."*

There needs to be a system of hatred in place that creates a network of norms, assumptions, behaviors, and policies. At various times in history, society's support to those holding government offices created a system which allowed hate to grow without resistance into the violence we witness in places around the world today.

One example of society's systematic support can be seen in United States' history. The government's atmosphere of division with a sustained societal support created an environment where lynching was an acceptable form of terror that lasted many decades. Southern hatred toward Blacks rose from the desire to maintain supremacy combined with the fear of living among freed Blacks who were no longer restrained by the institution of slavery.

In the late 1800s, the Southern Democrats, a group of Southern Congressmen who were also known as the Dixiecrats, created a political platform naming Blacks as the cause of the South's troubles. The Southern Democrats insisted Blacks had to be disenfranchised, separated, and forced to be kept in 'their place'.

At the end of the Civil War, the South's elected officials were allowed to determine for their respective states what the relationships between the races would look like. Not surprisingly, white leaders did what they could to maintain the status quo. Additionally, there was nothing done by the U.S. government to prevent the Confederate veterans from maintaining their relationships and views about the cause of the Civil War. This included putting pressure on southern schools to use history textbooks that portrayed Confederates as honorable, valiant, and fighting for freedom.

In the late 1800s and the early 1900s, children were also placed into clubs and organizations which celebrated the antebellum South and perpetuated views defeated by the Civil War. One such organization was the Children of the Confederacy, which was an auxiliary of the United Daughters of the Confederacy. Children basically became members of the organization from birth until they turned eighteen. The organization allowed adults to teach their white supremacy ideologies to their children.

With nothing to stop the spread of southern pride and their views that slavery was not a horrible institution, subsequent generations were indoctrinated that Whites were a superior race, that Blacks needed to be controlled for their own good and the good of society, and that alternate ideas were dismissed as lies. Those views became the "Jim Crow" system which created a pariah class of individuals who had no real rights. The Jim Crow system and the controls that system put into place created an atmosphere which allowed for continued societal support of lynching.

Between the 1880s until World War II, the conservative estimate that 4,700 people were lynched in the United States. Of these, seventy-three percent were Blacks and eighty percent occurred in the South. Of those occurring in the South, eighty-three percent were Black—approximately 3,200 people. It is estimated that a tenth of those killings were mass spectacles that included drawn-out torture, mutilation, burning, and/or dismemberment. The lynchers would often leave the body on display for hours or even days, and sometimes with a sign, as a message to others in the black community.

Some of the participants in a lynching may have erroneously thought they served justice and ensured community safety through honorable service. Bystanders of a lynching sometimes showed their support by shooting the body or taking pictures. Other times, bystanders were complicit in the violence by living their lives as if the lynching was not morally wrong. The spectacle lynching also served as a reminder there was no limit to what southern Whites would do to southern Blacks.

Lynching parties, even small ones, were often made up of rural and urban working-class citizens. While small, perhaps unsupported parties often committed a lynching in secrecy, mass mobs included people from all levels of society and were quite public.

In addition to men from all societal levels of the community present at a lynching, it was not uncommon for mothers and their children to attend and, in at least one instance, assist. In a lynching in 1919 in Vicksburg, Mississippi, women and several children were witnessed pouring gasoline on a man. The fact that respectable citizens participated gave the spectacle lynching an aura of "popular justice" legitimacy.

According to Berg, one lyncher professed, *"When we left home tonight our wives, daughters, and sisters kissed us goodbye and told us to do our duty, and we're trying to do it as citizens."*

The hate displayed towards Blacks was not a case of a handful of southern people but of a society who believed Blacks were inferior and the only way to "keep them in line" was to have public lynchings. Hate and violence became an acceptable part of society.

French sociologist, Emile Durkheim (1858-1917) created the term "social facts" to explain the practices that continue due to force of habit. The idea is that people become socialized to have the same ideals and beliefs as their predecessors through social integration. In the case of the South during the era of lynching, southern whites were socialized to believe in their dominance. With spectacle lynching where children were to be present, a method for maintaining dominance and the habit of dominance enforcement can be seen.

Lynching support not only came from the community, but also from media and published research. In 1901, Harvard scientist Nathaniel Southgate published a paper in which he condemned mob rule but excluded lynching from his condemnation. Southgate argued a lynching was carried out by *"decent men of American law-abiding type."* He equated lynching to legal executions and not *"a sign of real lawlessness, nor of a people given to savage outburst of fury."* His writings supported all lynching, by not classifying them as mob murder, but as a legal necessity.

There are numerous instances in which the media helped fuel support for lynching. One of the myths used to justify violence against Blacks was that black men were a moral threat to white

America, and white women in particular. Several works of fiction and pseudoscientific tracts helped spread that narrative. Newspapers portrayed black men as monstrous killers and sexual predators for which the only fitting punishment was torture. Before the invention of the radio, people received current information and news via newspapers. The information provided in newspapers was seen as factual. The newsprint's portrayal of black men and support for their torture lent further credence to the horrific actions against Blacks.

There were cases in which misinformation in newspapers directly led to spectacle lynching. In one case, a local paper insinuated the killers of a white man were part of a larger black conspiracy ring who had also killed several other Whites. The news article alluded to a Black uprising resulting in a group of two hundred men lynching two innocent black men as a "necessary precaution" to protect all Whites from the threat. If it had not been for the newspaper's article spreading misinformation about a Black uprising and inflaming hatred and fear, the two men would likely not have been murdered.

While the community and media lent support to lynching, the lack of action and complicity of law enforcement officers gave the vigilantes added encouragement that their actions were socially acceptable within their communities. In many instances of "justice" lynching, the community's law officers did nothing to stop the mob from taking the victim, and in some cases would assist with the lynching.

In 1916 in Waco, Texas, a black man, Jesse Washington, was convicted of killing a white woman. Even though plans to lynch the convicted man were well known throughout the community, law officers did nothing to stop the mob. In fact, the sheriff ordered his men to stand down and allowed a photographer to take photos of the lynching from City Hall. The photos of Jesse's burned body hanging from the tree were later sold as souvenirs.

Ten thousand people were said to have watched the torture, hanging, and burning of the convicted man. That is only one example of many in which law officers did nothing to stop unlawful lynching from occurring. There are even more examples of law officers assisting in lynching.

The overarching opinions of law enforcement officers in areas of the south where lynching was prevalent were best exemplified by the quote attributed to a late nineteenth-century police chief regarding the three types of homicides.

He declared, *"If a nigger kills a white man, that's a murder. If a white man kills a nigger, that's justifiable homicide. If a nigger kills a nigger, that's one less nigger."*

It is not surprising that the lynching numbers in each area had a direct correlation to law enforcement's protection of minorities.

Protecting lynchers did not stop with those who wore a badge. Often the coroner declared "death by parties unknown" in their reports. They marked that on the death certificates even though the lynchers' names were known. In the case in Waco, Texas, pictures clearly identified those participating in the lynching. The lynchers did nothing to conceal their identities as they were confident there would be no repercussion of their crimes. If law enforcement did nothing to arrest those who committed what today would be considered murder, it gave lynching the aura of legitimacy and legality.

The court systems were sometimes complicit in "legalizing" killing a black man through mob-dominated trials. The trials were often done in one day, and the jury often remained in the courtroom while making their decision. There was little concern about the trial outcome being overturned, or for the case to ever get close to being heard by the Supreme Court. The legal system's aiding of the violence added another layer of systemic support.

The last level of support, and one that added the most credence to those who committed violence and murder, came from the people in government and leadership positions. Throughout the time of spectacle lynching, legitimacy to the lynchers' actions was provided by speakers, to governors, to the U.S. presidents, as leaders and elected officials played an important role in shaping and influencing society. Their societal group views direct the actions of those within a society. Leaders define who is the enemy and engage in actions that encourage violence. These leaders use propaganda, sometimes in conjunction with media outlets, to intensify negative stereotypes and inflame hostility. During "bad" times or when there's a need for misdirection to solidify or divide a community, leaders will often help identify a select group toward which hate and violence "should" be targeted.

In 1899 in Georgia, there was a peak in lynching which could be partially attributed to one woman, Rebecca Latimer Felton. Felton was a woman defender of lynching laws. She wrote a speech in which she blamed white men for not doing all they could to protect white women from black men.

In her speech, she articulated, *"If it needs lynching to protect a woman's dearest possession from the ravenous human beasts, then I say lynch a thousand times a week, if necessary."*

Felton used the myth of rape dangers by a black man to fuel lynching. Her feelings were summed up after a lynching in April 1899, when she stated a shot dog was *"more worth of sympathy than a lynched black man."*

At the state level, there were many southern politicians who perpetrated Black stereotypes, supported lynching, and in some cases even participated. A leading Mississippi politician was quoted as saying Blacks were *"lazy, lying, lustful animals which no conceivable amount of training can transform into a tolerable citizen."*

In many cases, governors did nothing to encourage local law enforcement to track down and arrest those who participated in a lynching. In fact, in 1919 Mississippi Governor Theodore Bilbo told the National Association for the Advancement of Colored People (NAACP) to "go to Hell" after four black youths were lynched and the group asked the governor to act.

When asked to prosecute potential mob leaders, South Carolina Governor Coleman Livingston Blease refused to do so. He declared he would not send the militia to protect a child rapist, and if forced would resign and lead the mob.

He would later say, *"Whenever the Constitution comes between me and the virtue of white women, I say to Hell with the Constitution."*

The states had authority to stop the hateful and violent lynching, and while some states had anti-lynching laws, they often made it clear, particularly in the South, they would not do anything to penalize those acts.

While it would have been nice to have state support for lynching to end, there had been federal support to include Congress and the president. The first attempt to federally stop lynching was made in 1891 by President Harrison after eleven Italians were lynched in

New Orleans while awaiting trial. The impetus for an anti-lynching law was not due to lynching occurring nationwide, but rather the lynching of the Italians caused an international incident. While the law Harrison submitted would have been for all lynching, the final bill only addressed foreign nationals.

Prior to 1910, eight attempts were made to pass anti-lynching laws for lynching prevalent in the South—all died in Congress. Many of the bills died due to opposition from Southern Democrats who filibustered to prevent a vote. Many argued the law would infringe on state's rights or that a federal law was unnecessary. They also argued the rape myth to support the need for lynching and mob violence, essentially calling the lynching 'justice'. The fight against anti-lynching laws tacitly supported the lynching parties.

Support of violent ideologies from the highest office in the United States further justified advocates of lynching as a form of punishment. When President Woodrow Wilson praised the movie, *Birth of a Nation*, as *"like writing history with lightnin',"* he further emboldened advocates of lynching. The movie perpetuated the South's rape myth used to justify lynching and portrayed the Ku Klux Klan as heroes protecting white citizens, particularly women. President Wilson's praise came as community leaders condemned the movie for the same reasons.

While not directly supporting lynching, President Theodore Roosevelt upheld the view rape by black men was one of the main causes of lynching. Roosevelt asserted, *"The worst enemy of the negro race is the negro criminal type...and every reputable colored man owes it as his first duty to himself to hunt down that criminal with all his soul and strength."*

Throughout history, other presidents had little or nothing to say against lynching plaguing the South, and thus gave tacit support.

While lynching occurred other than in the southern states, support for lynching elsewhere was scarce. After a lynching in Pennsylvania, serious effort was made to track down the lynchers. That led to the arrest of eight people, which included the police chief and his deputy for their neglect to uphold the law. In 1920, the Minnesota governor sent in the National Guard resulting in the indictment of more than a dozen people, including a photographer who was charged with displaying "indiscreet and obscene pictures". In

September of that year, two of the lynchers were convicted of rioting and sentenced to up to five years in prison, and a juvenile was sent to serve time in a reformatory. The negative reaction to lynching in those states was diametrically opposite to that in the South.

Southern lynching showed signs of losing support during and after World War I, following a lynching frenzy of returning black soldiers. The lynching of the soldiers in Georgia caused condemnation throughout the United States. Even President Woodrow Wilson, who had previously shown apathy toward the South's racial views, admonished the South for contributing to German lies about the United States in terms of lynching. Southerners ignored the lynching as a societal issue, instead placed blame on German spies attempting to start an insurrection among Blacks. Other than the lynching incident with the Italians, it was the first time southern lynching received widespread condemnation. Condemnation was short lived, as there were decades more of lynchings.

In the 1940s, spectacle lynching came to an end. Southern support for such public events evaporated. Support for racial violence also declined but did not vanish. While spectacle lynching declined, evidence that secret killings rose in its place does not exist, indicating an overall decline in societal support for such violence. While social condemnation of violence increased, individual frustration also increased among those who disagreed with society's acceptance of minorities. So, while those who committed violent actions against others could no longer rely on community support, social condemnation did not eliminate their hatred.

Events around the 1946 Georgia gubernatorial elections made that apparent. Candidate Eugene Talmadge told Blacks to stay away from the polls. After his victory, widespread violent incidents against Blacks increased. In one instance, two couples were murdered. The country's changing attitudes were displayed when President Harry S. Truman asked the Department of Justice to investigate the murders. While the FBI was met with a wall of silence, investigators were able to arrest some men for the murders. The accused men were later acquitted by an all-white jury. So, while the case showed attitudes were changing and acceptance of violence was no longer tolerated by the higher levels of government, there remained some who would not convict Whites for crimes against Blacks.

In the 1950s, only nine percent of households had a television set. In the 1960s, that percentage rose to ninety percent, which helped change society's views on racial violence. That brought images of cruelty to nonviolent civil rights activists into our homes. Instead of reading about fire hoses and police dogs being turned against activists, television delivered violent images to Americans in other parts of the country. That pressured the southern states to make changes and further ostracized the hate-fueled criminals committing the previously supported violence against Blacks and civil rights activists. By the mid-1960s, southern Whites grew tired of the violence and further pushed back on those criminals. While violence did not completely disappear by the 1970s, it became marginalized, and those committing race crimes could no longer rely on community support or the silence of their peers.

Starting in the 1980s, the change in society's support of racial violence saw major changes. In one case, two Klan members were convicted of killing a black man after another black man was set free due to a hung jury. In 1997, for the first time since 1913, a white man was executed for the killing of a black man, and the all-white jury awarded seven million dollars to the mother of the victim.

In 2009, after the brutal killings of James Byrd Jr. in Jasper, Texas and of Matthew Shepard in Laramie, Wyoming in 1998, Congress passed the Federal Hate Crime Law. After over 200 attempts and 130 years, the Emmett Till Anti-lynching Act, named after the fourteen-year-old black boy who was murdered for asking a white girl on a date, was finally passed by Congress on March 7, 2022 and signed into law by President Biden on March 29th. While the laws have not stopped hate-fueled violence, they have made hate crimes not merely a socially unacceptable form of justice, but illegal.

These examples of the United States' era of racially motivated lynching and the subsequent decline of society's acceptance of lynching demonstrates how hate is controlled by a society. Hate feeds on hate, creating a feedback loop which causes escalation and spread of hate. A phenomenon known as the "Kristallnacht Effect" (Night of Broken Glass), so called from a night of violence against Jews by Germany's Nazi party in November 1938 is the idea that people who commit a hate crime against another race are vindicated because the victims deserved it, and the attackers are justified in striking them again. If hate crimes are not stopped, they lead to more hate crimes. It produces a group-thought that the victims were justifiably attacked because they must be enemies.

Professor Ehud Sprinzak, Israeli counter-terrorism specialist and expert in far-right Jewish groups developed the "Iceberg Model" to explain the escalation of hate-fueled violence and the support of those who commit hate crimes. The model theorizes *"that terrorism or an act of terrorism is only the tip of an iceberg. An iceberg has only ten percent of its total mass above the water...the analogy is that underneath (or, on a timeline, before) the actual terrorist attack there is a great deal going on."* As prior acts are ignored by law enforcement and supported, either openly or through silence, by the community, discontent grows within the iceberg, wherein those with the most hate move to the top. Those who are visible at the tip of the iceberg are the ones who commit acts of hate-fueled violence. If society and law enforcement worked to stop the underlying hateful rhetoric against peoples of another race or culture, the rise to high levels of violence and hate within society would be stymied.

Racially based lynchings show how allowing uncontrolled hate-fueled violence to exist in 'the open' can lead to more hate and violence—and is one of the best examples of hate progression from one extreme to the other. As we go through a time of increased hate, it's hard to see how the trend can be reversed. We stopped the spread of the worse hate and violence in our country, so the ability is there. It would be nice if it were as simple as developing a vaccine, but it's more complicated than that.

Much like a virus, one way to slow hate's spread is by forcing it into isolation, which essentially is what happened when hate-based violence became unacceptable to most of the society. Quarantining hate is achieved by society condemning hate and violence. When hate is seen as socially unacceptable, hate is rarely allowed to be openly shown. The easy avenues of spreading hate are closed off, and those who wish to recruit people in their hate of others get little or no support from their community, society, and its leaders. Societal isolation of hate and of those who committed hate-based violence allowed the granddaughter of a man whose actions of hate were significant, to grow up quarantined from that hatred of others and not have that hate passed on to her.

Chapter 2 ~ Let Me Introduce Myself

My life is my message. —Mahatma Gandhi

I am about to take you on a journey using my personal story to explain why I believe something can be done to help limit the hate we've been witnessing. To do this, I feel the need to tell you about myself, so you can better understand the journey I took to get here. Nothing is distinctive about me or my life, other than who I discovered my grandfather to be. But even that's not all that unique, as many people have skeletons in their family closets they wish were not there. To see how hate's spread can be stopped with isolation, you must understand how I grew up and who I am today.

My father was born in Wisconsin but grew up in Cleveland. He dropped out of school to join the Army when he was seventeen. After he served out his enlistment, my father returned to Cleveland, doing different jobs before becoming a mail carrier—a job he did until he retired.

My mother was born in Lithuania and came to the United States and the Cleveland area when she was around eight. She went to a trade school after high school graduation to become a secretary at a legal firm, where she worked until my brother was born.

My parents met in a bar, and because my father was not completely truthful about his age, they started dating. My father is younger than my mother by over a year, which was younger than the men she generally wanted to date. They eventually got married and started a family.

My brother was born first in 1966 and had medical issues as a baby and young child. He also had issues with making friends. If he was not watching game shows on our one television set, he spent most of his time in his room. In 2001, he was diagnosed with Asperger's Syndrome, now known as high functioning autism. My brother's diagnosis explained much of the difficulties he had in school and with making friends. He became active in the school's theatre group and was inducted in the local thespian society.

I was born five-and-a-half years after my brother. Between the age difference and my brother's difficulties, we were not close growing up, but we would do things together from time to time. We became closer when we got older.

My parents moved to Elyria, Ohio with my brother before I was born. They wanted to move from the Cleveland neighborhood to a place they thought would be better to raise their family. The city of Elyria was a typical midwestern city. It is located thirty miles west of Cleveland and has a population of around 55,000 people—which was approximately the population when I grew up there. The city's demographics is seventy-six percent White, sixteen percent Black, and small percentages of other racial groups. Elyria was a blue-collar town with only twenty-five percent of the population having at least an associate degree, according to the 2021 demographics statistics. While I was not able to track down the city's statistics for education levels when I was growing up, I doubt the percentage was higher. I believe it was probably lower.

My father was a mail carrier in a city nearer Cleveland but thought the commute would be worth living in the better place. He left the house before I was up for school. There were days when my father wouldn't get home until late, especially around the holidays when the mail volume was much greater. My mother stayed at home until I started school full day in first grade, at which time she took a job as a floral designer.

The house I grew up in was in a typical middle-class neighborhood. Houses were separated by a one-car driveway and a strip of grass. Every house had a tree on the strip of grass between the sidewalk and street. In fact, my city referred to that section as 'the tree lawn'. My city was separated from the next by railroad tracks which ran behind the houses where the street formed a horseshoe. The sound of the train and its horn were part of my childhood memories. I swear the engineers blew their horns more on summer nights when our windows were open. During the summers, I also heard trucks on the Ohio Turnpike a mile away. I heard conversations from the neighbors' houses until some got window air-conditioning units.

I am amazed we lived in a house under 1,000 square feet with only one bathroom. The smaller house may partially explain why I spent most of my time outside regardless of the season. Many of the neighborhood kids would spend most of their time playing outside. The kids I played with were mainly boys, who were the only kids my age on my block. I am not sure if I was a tomboy because of that or if

I naturally was a tomboy, but mainly growing up around boys was not a problem for me. When we were younger, we rode our big wheels up and down the sidewalks and spun out in people's driveways. As we got older, we played tape ball, tag football, swimming, snowball wars, and anything else we could find to occupy our time.

One of my first friends was a boy who lived a street over from mine. We met at the monkey bars set up between the houses on the two streets. I never knew who owned them. Some kids gathered there to play instead of going to the small park at the other end of the street. After we met, we became inseparable.

We hung out just about every day and spent the night at each other's houses. He was the reason I played soccer since I wanted to do what he did. Our friendship stalled when his family moved to a different neighborhood while we were still in elementary school. He went to a different elementary school after he moved. We went to the same junior high, but we had no similar classes, which put an end to our friendship. He was the first and probably strongest friendship of my childhood.

After he moved away, I hung out with some of the boys on my street. They went to private Baptist schools, but we spent most of our time outside school together. I am not sure their parents liked them spending so much time with a tomboy who was a Catholic, and a non-practicing one at that. Regardless of how their parents felt about me, we spent a lot of time together because I had a pool in my backyard, and my participation allowed for the right number of people to play most games.

During the summer, most of our time was spent in my above-ground pool. I joke that I am surprised I did not develop gills and webbed fingers and toes. We often played 'Marco Polo', which I am sure drove our neighbors crazy hearing "Marco!" and "Polo!" shouted for hours just about every summer day. Our houses didn't have central air, so everyone had their windows open and would've clearly heard us. We generally got out of the pool only to eat.

I paid for all that pool time in the sun later in life when I got diagnosed with melanoma. But during that time, it was a fun, cooling way to pass the hot summer days.

During the winters, we spent time building forts, having snowball fights, and playing board games. When Atari was created, we played video games. Our fort-building and snowball fights sometimes got serious. We soaked snowballs in gutter water and buried them to freeze.

One year, an older neighbor and I came up with a plan to prevent our fort from being knocked down by our "enemies". We ran a hose from his house and wet down each layer of the fort before adding more snow. It created a solid wall of ice that was over five feet tall. No one was able to knock that fort down. The downside to our engineering was that our snow fort was on the tree lawn and blocked my parents' view when they pulled out our driveway. It was sometime in April before the fort melted. I continued hearing complaints about trouble seeing around my fort until it melted down to a lower height.

While I did have a few kids to play with, I often felt like an outsider. I was not always included in my friends' activities. I at times saw them walk past my house to go do something or heard them playing at the house next door. It was hard on me to see my friends go off to do other things without me. I sometimes laid on my bed and listened to them play basketball next door, knowing they didn't want me to join them. Sometimes, I convinced my brother to play a board game or cards. I did whatever I could to pass the time until my friends included me in their activities.

The part of my youth I look back on with the most fondness was when I played soccer. I fell in love with the sport and looked forward to games and summer camps. I learned to play every position but spent most of my time playing goalie. Even though I typically was the shortest person on the field and had a vertical leap of only a couple of inches, I held my own by being aggressive and having good reflexes.

When I found myself with no one to hang out with, I often took my soccer ball into the yard to practice dribbling or juggling. It gave me something to focus on other than the idea the other kids were off doing other things. I don't know the reason I was sometimes excluded, but it may have been because I was a girl and they wanted to hang out without me. Regardless, it was difficult being the outsider watching others having fun.

I basically was a typical kid who tried to be good and have fun. I generally did not get into trouble, but, like any other kid, it happened. I got into trouble with my parents if I did not come home when the streetlights came on, did not do a chore I was asked to do, or if I didn't tell my parents where I was going. I also got in trouble for fighting with other kids. I had a bad temper growing up and often got into fights. Most were standard squabbles over being 'out' or 'safe' in tape ball or whether someone was 'down' in football, but there were fights that stemmed from being angry about being left out or when kids made fun of my brother.

I also had some issues with peer pressure that got me to do things that hurt others. One incident that occurred on the bus in junior high has stuck with me after decades. During my eighth-grade year, my assigned seat on the bus was the first seat by the door and was shared with two other students. One of them was someone I had been in school with since kindergarten and the other was a student with cerebral palsy. While I didn't like riding the bus with three in the seat, it was not a long trip to school, and I could tolerate it. My classmate since kindergarten did not like it at all.

This classmate played the violin, and I played the alto saxophone. There were days when we would both have our instruments with us, which would make it an even tighter fit. One day, my classmate told me to put my instrument case a different way so it would take up more room to try to force the other student to move. The bus driver saw what was happening and informed us we either find a way to allow the other student to sit or the instruments would have to go.

I hated the look on the student's face as she took her seat next to me. I knew what it felt like to be excluded, but I had gone along with the scheme. It was not often I let peer pressure make me do something I regretted, but until my self-confidence became stronger, I had difficulties standing up for what I thought was right.

In school, much to my parents' surprise, I was seen as the quiet, shy student who did well in all my work. For some reason, even though I was quiet, I had teachers, especially in elementary school, who took a liking to me. I became what was referred to as the 'teacher's pet'. I was asked to clean the chalkboard, help with grading, and would sometimes spend recess talking with my teacher instead of playing.

I loved going to school and learning new things. While I was not at the top in my classes in grades, I was known as being part of the "smart" group. In elementary school, I was put in a program called the 'Program for the Academically Talented (PAT)'. We had a special time during the day when we went into a different room to work on projects or logic puzzles. I was part of the program through junior high and then was in the 'honors classes' in high school. While I enjoyed the challenge the programs gave me, it caused a barrier between some of the friends I had had since kindergarten and me. Even in the programs, when we were told to pair up, I often was the odd person out—which I did not completely mind. I enjoyed working on puzzles by myself, but sometimes I would've liked to have been paired with a classmate.

When I was in school, my speech impediments caused me to stand out from my classmates, not in a good way. The impediment I had in elementary school was a hard time pronouncing certain words. Many children spend time with speech therapists in kindergarten and possibly into the first grade. I went to speech therapists through at least second grade, and still some words remain difficult for me. I remember being in a small room with a therapist as she tried to help me correctly pronounce words. When I was in junior high, I developed a stammer. I have figured out ways to hide and control my stammer, but to develop one during a socially awkward time was difficult for me. I found it easier to not talk than to risk being teased about stammering. Since I did not talk much anyway, it didn't raise many questions with my peers or teachers.

Even before I got to high school, there was no question as to whether I was going to go to college. Between doing well in math and science and having an aunt who taught electrical engineering at a major university, I was pushed towards engineering. There was talk about me attending the college where my aunt taught, but the first question asked when attending the university's engineering camp was if I was her niece, I decided to go elsewhere. I ended up attending the University of Toledo for electrical engineering.

The jump from high school to college was not an easy one for me. Being academically challenged for the first time was one of my toughest hardships. Throughout high school, I never had to study for tests, so I didn't develop any study skills. I quickly found out I was going to have to study to succeed, especially in the engineering program. I never got good at studying, but I was able to get through the program and graduate.

It took me five years to complete my Bachelor of Science in electrical engineering, with four of those years spent living in the dorms. I rarely stayed on campus during the weekends when my floormates partied. Even when I could legally drink alcohol, I didn't drink enough to get a buzz. I didn't enjoy going to parties. Being around people who were drunk wasn't something I enjoyed, so I went to my parents' house on weekends. By that time in my life, I often made myself an outsider to avoid feeling yoyoed between being included and excluded by others. I found in a way emotionally it was easier to stay an outsider.

While I kept myself from forming close relationships, I took an interest in learning about other people, especially those from cultures I had not had an opportunity to know in my hometown. College was the first time I was introduced to people from other socioeconomic backgrounds and countries. I had limited opportunities to meet people (mainly adults) from other countries while playing soccer and going to soccer camps. I enjoyed interacting with non-American citizens I met in college. Part of my enjoyment was learning about their countries as I thought my chances of traveling outside the United States was small. I never considered I'd live outside the Cleveland area, let alone be able to travel the world.

A few weeks after graduation, I attended the Society of Women Engineers conference in Pittsburgh. I went because I was an officer the previous school year, and I thought it would be fun. More importantly, they had a job fair. My mother had told me I was not allowed to get a job more than two hours away from home. During the job fair, I interviewed with a company called Applied Materials, which was based in California and had a site in Texas. I interviewed to experience a professional interview. I think because I didn't care about getting the job, I was relaxed and did well on the behavioral-based interview. Later, I passed by the company's table at the fair. My interviewer told me I had done a great job.

When I returned home, I asked my mother what mode of transportation was used for the stipulated 'two hours away' job-distance guideline. A few weeks later, I had an offer extended to me—I was heading to Austin, Texas for my first post-graduate career.

I found myself several states away from my family and anyone I knew, beyond one college classmate who also got hired by the company. I previously spent time away from my family, but not for an extended period. I was not only beginning a career, but I was also doing it all alone in an unfamiliar place.

After spending a few years in the company's manufacturing department, I moved into software deployment. As part of the project, I traveled to other countries where my company had offices. Not only did I travel to countries I thought I'd never be fortunate enough to visit, but my company also paid for it. My first overseas trip fortunately was to Newcastle, England. Other than trying to get in a car on the wrong side and the sun never really setting, I didn't experience much culture shock.

I learned on one trip to England how different perspectives of historic events are. In the United States, in almost every United States history course we thoroughly learn about the thirteen original colonies and the American Revolution. When I visited the Royal Marines Museum, my co-workers and I were amused to see the American Revolution, or as they called it the Colony Revolt, covered by two plaques stuck in the corner behind other displays. It was a good lesson in how one event can be portrayed two different ways. It made me further explore historical as well as current events.

My work took me to Israel, Taiwan, China, India, South Korea, and several other countries where I spent two to three weeks. I spent my weekends seeing the countries' sights and enjoying meals with co-workers' families. I had dinner in Israel with a Jewish family, lunch with a Korean co-worker in her apartment near our office, and visited Hindu temples in India followed by dinner at a co-worker's family home. While working with people allows one to learn about them, spending personal time in their home allows an invaluable glimpse into their lives. It gave me the opportunity to see their homes are not that different from families I knew growing up—the food, accents, language, and decor were a bit different.

A major shift in my life's direction, and I presume for many people was 9/11. I arrived in California on the evening of September 10th. Because of the time difference, I was still sleeping when the day's events occurred. I found out what had happened after I went to the hotel's lobby for breakfast. Like many people on business trips probably did, I left that day by car and headed back to Texas. During that trip I deeply thought about my career. When driving through the Arizona and New Mexico deserts with little-to-no radio reception, there's not much to do but think. During that trip I considered pursuing an advanced degree. After looking at my options, I decided on an MBA in global management from the University of Phoenix. At the time, it was the only program available that would accommodate my work travel.

A few months after finishing my MBA, I requested information about their Doctor of Management Organizational Leadership program. I joke that I thought the person to whom I spoke was a former military recruiter because I called for information, and by the time I got off the phone, I was halfway signed up for the doctorate program.

Completing my doctorate was not easy, not only because of the rigor of the program but I was laid off from Applied Materials. I managed to find another job at a small aviation maintenance software company but after a couple of years was let go.

I finished up my doctorate in November of 2009 while still unemployed. In my experience, finding a job when you have a doctorate degree is not easy. I managed to acquire a few contractor jobs. I taught management classes as an adjunct instructor with the University of Phoenix at their Austin and Killeen campuses. Serving as an adjunct professor propelled me to apply at a university. It was a bit of a *Hail Mary* since I had been unemployed for well over a year and in desperation thought someone might hire me. I submitted applications to numerous universities. The University of Arkansas at Fort Smith offered me a position.

When I began teaching full-time, I wasn't sure if I would like it. I am not one who likes doing repetitive work. I found, however, I enjoyed teaching and watching the students' growth.

I am known as a challenging professor, but many have come to see I care about them and their future successes. My classes prepare students to be supervisors and managers. While I enjoy teaching most of the classes, the one I enjoy most is my diversity class. It is an opportunity for my students, many of whom have never lived anywhere but Arkansas, to explore other cultures. On the first day of class, I warn them we cover topics they may not be able to talk about at their family's holiday meal. I see it as my duty to teach students to look beyond stereotypes. While I know I cannot and will not change how all students see others, I am hopeful most will leave my class with a different perspective or at least a planted seed that will later grow.

I have lived through rough times. My trials made it difficult for me to build relationships and trust others. I've had moments of being excluded from activities, treated differently because I was a female in male-dominated areas, and made to feel unwelcome. I've had both amazing managers and some who were toxic. I learned a great deal at times I felt most unpleasantly treated. My experiences taught me to not make anyone else feel the way I had felt. I try not to judge others based on how they look, their religion or lack thereof, or how much money they do or don't have. I try to see them by how they treat others and who they are as human beings. I cannot say I'm flawless at that. I feel I have room for improvement, but I have come far from being the kid who fought and who was pressured into making others feel bad. The thought of people getting harmed for their beliefs, their skin's color, or their nationality pains me. My feelings toward those who harm others different than them include disgust and anger. That made dealing with my grandfather's story hard for me.

Chapter 3 ~ The Grandfather I Knew

To be human is to have a collection of memories that tells you who you are and how you got there —Rosecrans Baldwin

Everyone who remembers their grandparents has memories when they think about them. When I think back on the grandfather I grew up knowing, I remember his authoritative manner, his Husky, the big backyard with the large oak tree I climbed, and the low-flying airplanes approaching to land at Cleveland Hopkins International Airport. Those are the images that come to mind. There are also silly little memories, like the multicolor pen he always had near where he sat in the living room, the lilac bush that grew at the edge of the porch that created a wonderful smell with the breeze, and the candy bowl particularly with butterscotch ones I came to love. The man himself seemed larger than life in terms of how he affected the house's atmosphere. His personality and his moods set the tone for everything that happened in the house.

My memories of my grandfather center around his house as he rarely left it. That included visiting us at our house. I only recall him visiting once when we had a cookout. My parents set up a small TV on the patio, so my grandfather could watch a boxing match. The only other time I remember seeing him away from his home was when he came to one of my recreational soccer games. He had managed a soccer team in Lithuania and said he wanted to see me play at least once. He did not stay long after the game, though.

Since he didn't come to us, we drove from Elyria to Cleveland almost every Sunday to visit. It was an expected part of the week. Only when a conflicting commitment occurred on Sunday, did we not take the thirty-minute drive into Cleveland. If we did miss a Sunday, we rarely missed the next one. We also celebrated every Christmas, New Year's Day, and Easter at his home.

We visited my mother's father more often than my father's mother. Since they didn't live far apart, we sometimes visited both on the same day. I never understood why we visited Grandfather more often than my grandmother. My best guess was my grandfather seemed much more demanding. My grandmother never seemed to lose her temper and was the type of person who treated strangers like a dear friend. She found it amusing when my friend (who had previously visited grandmother and eaten a few of her homemade chocolate chip cookies) rummaged through her kitchen for more on a following visit. Had he done that at my grandfather's house, I doubt my grandfather would've found my friend's behavior appropriate.

The overall feeling at my grandfather's house was different than that of my grandmother's in that my grandmother was more relaxed and, while she had rules, hers were not as stringently enforced. Based on my grandfather's general reaction to certain situations, I believe he would have openly shared his dislike for my friend had my friend behaved in a similar way in my grandfather's house.

I perceived my grandfather's house as a fort, which, after learning more about him, made sense. A solid wall of tall bushes bordered his front yard. A walkway leading to the porch was the wall's only opening. A large pine tree, which was a Christmas tree when my mom was a child, blocked his house from being seen from the road. Even in his backyard, tall bushes created a wall between his and his neighbors' yards. When I was a kid, it felt cool to walk into that natural fortress. In retrospect, I strongly suspect the bushes were planted for privacy, to keep people out and block them from seeing into his house and yard.

Fond memories I have of my grandfather tend to revolve around how special he made me feel. Kissing my grandfather's cheek was the first thing my brother, mother, and I did upon entering his house. I was the only one he allowed to kiss him on his left cheek. He told me his left cheek was my side and only my side.

My grandfather often treated me differently from his other grandkids. He had four grandchildren. I was the youngest and the only girl. I think that's why my grandfather doted on me more than the others. Hence, him allowing only me to kiss his left cheek made me feel special and created warm feelings toward him when I was younger and continued into adulthood. Who wouldn't enjoy feeling like their grandparent's favorite?

Presumably, outings to my grandfather's home were like other people's visits to theirs. While some may have developed friendships with their grandparents' neighborhood children, or maybe visits coincided with cousins' visits, there wasn't much to do during our visits. My grandfather and his neighbors didn't interact while we visited, so if they had kids, I wasn't aware of them. I couldn't tell you anything about my grandfather's neighbors except that one had a Saint Bernard I could see from the oak tree I climbed.

Most visits to grandfather's house were what I consider normal, where the adults got lost in discussions and then maybe help my grandfather with house repairs or cleaning. Sometimes Mom cut my grandfather's hair. Grandfather had board games upstairs, but my brother typically was not interested in playing and the adults were too busy. Grandfather's pool table was in the basement, but my brother and I couldn't use it without adult supervision for fear we might damage it.

I had to find other ways to entertain myself. When I was little, I occupied time by sliding down the second-story stairwell on my butt. I slid until the adults got annoyed or my butt hurt too much. If the weather was nice, I went into the backyard and sat in the oak tree. From there, I hoped to see the neighbor's St. Bernard. If I had been more into books when I was younger, it would've been a good way to pass the time. Instead, I tried to pass the time without causing trouble until we left, which I successfully did, most of the time.

Since my mother's family was from Lithuania one might think they spoke Lithuanian or that they would teach their language to my brother and me. The only time I heard the language spoken was when my mother and grandfather discussed private matters like birthday or Christmas presents. Otherwise, the Lithuanian language was not used and much of their Lithuanian culture was not discussed. The only Lithuanian traditions observed were during our holiday meals.

I only remember the holiday meals at my grandfather's house. While Lithuanian culture and traditions weren't often discussed, I felt holiday meals were important because they reminded my grandfather of life in Lithuania. I knew we'd be at my grandfather's for every holiday, except Thanksgiving, which we celebrated with my father's family.

Holiday meals in the traditional Lithuanian fashion were all-day affairs. That meant we nibbled all day at a table full of food and had plenty of liquor to fuel discussions. Discussions during those meals lasted for hours and mainly centered around current events. I didn't hear any talk about Lithuania or any family there. In fact, I only heard about our extended family in Lithuania a couple of times, and only when my grandfather and mother discussed presents for them at Christmastime. While I was young, Lithuania was behind the Iron Curtain, so they were restricted on what they could send. Other than those few conversations, they never mentioned Lithuania or their lives prior to coming to the United States. Those holiday meals were embedded in my memory, and I feel as if I learned the most about my grandfather during them.

My grandfather had transformed an old bedroom into his dining room. It had a table that sat six people, a smaller table next to my grandfather's chair that held a big, old vacuum-tube radio, and a well-stocked liquor cabinet. Needless to say, it was a tight squeeze. My chair sat next to my mother's, opposite the door. So, I was basically trapped in the room—which may have been on purpose since I had problems sitting still. The tight layout made it hard for me to leave when I got bored with adult conversation.

Once the table was ready, we went into the dining room and readied for our holiday feast. Our meals usually consisted of the same things: cold fried chicken (I know, it doesn't sound very eastern European, but we had it every holiday meal as it can be eaten cold), ham, cold salads, some kind of herring dish, and, many times, head cheese. My mother made us try a bite of everything before we could refuse it—except the head cheese. We never had to try head cheese because she didn't like it. It usually remained by my grandfather's plate.

For those who don't know what head cheese is, it's chopped meat from the head of a pig or calf in a jelly-like material, served cold. Think of a roasting pan after the meat has been removed and the remaining juices have cooled to a gelatin consistency. That's what head cheese looked like. As I've never tried it, I cannot say how it tastes. While there were other traditional Lithuanian dishes, head cheese was one that had an ethnic feel to it, due to its appearance.

Many people make dishes for celebrations because of fond memories of past meals. I wonder if head cheese was a dish my grandfather's family made during holidays, and it brought back fond memories.

Many families might have started their meals with a prayer and then passed around the food dishes. At my grandfather's, meals started with him preparing vodka shots for the adults. I was amazed at my grandfather's ability to pour vodka shots. Observing him was how I first learned about liquid's surface tension. Somehow, he managed to pour so the vodka was slightly higher than the shot glasses' rims. Once the shots were prepared, a toast was made and the adults 'threw back' their shots. My brother and I toasted with glasses of pop, usually 7-Up. We, however, did not test surface tension and kept our drinks' levels below the glass rim. Once the toast and shots were completed, the meal began.

Now, I've heard people fill their plates at most holiday meals. They eat their meal while having general discussions, and once everyone is finished eating (from thirty minutes to an hour), clean-up is done, and the rest of the celebration commenced in another room—maybe the living room.

It didn't happen like that at my grandfather's house. Holiday meals were an all-evening event which lasted two or more hours. Instead of filling our plates and eating all at once, we nibbled on food. The adults nibbled while drinking and talking.

One would think with several hours of drinking there would be a house full of drunk adults. With consistent nibbling of food, the impact of alcohol consumption was limited. My father spent a few holiday meals at my mother's house when they first started dating. When he attended his first meal, he didn't know to intersperse his eating and drinking. Being a young man recently out of the army, my father found out the hard way he couldn't keep up with my grandfather's drinking. I'm told it did not go well. That evening my father learned to nibble and sip. That's not to say my father should have been driving after our holiday meals, as I'm not sure he wouldn't have been considered impaired. But I never saw him as inebriated as he apparently was after his first meal with my mother's family.

My grandfather was strict on following traditions the correct way. For instance, a traditional dish for New Year's was meat pie. The cook hid a waxed paper-wrapped dime under the pie's top crust. At the New Year, the pie was cut into eight slices to represent God, country, family, and the family members, and handed out. The pieces were then checked for the dime. Whoever got the dime would have good luck in the new year. Because one looked for the dime at midnight, a phone call to wish a happy New Year was made and we waited to hear who got the dime.

Traditions and rules were important to my grandfather. He probably wouldn't be pleased that while we still have meat pie, we cut it during our New Year's Day meal. In fact, the pie isn't even made until that day, and we've been using puff pastry instead of phyllo, which he also may not have preferred. My grandfather felt our traditions needed to be consistent in order to maintain our customs.

Along the lines of traditions and rules, my grandfather was big on etiquette. In his house, you followed his rules—especially at the dinner table. He had a book on etiquette written by Emily Post, which he would retrieve if there were questions on the proper way of doing something, such as napkin placement. We were to hold our forks in our left hands, napkins in our laps, say "please" and "thank you," and ask permission to leave the table. It was breaking the last rule that got me in trouble with my grandfather. I don't recall any other lecture I got from him, except leaving the table without permission. It seems like an easy thing to do, ask for permission, but not after the adults got to debating things.

I quickly finished my meal and was then stuck in that small room with adults talking about politics, world events, or other boring topics. I had no desire to stay there for very long. I tried for as long as I could. I was often there longer than I really wanted to be as I waited for a break in their discussions so I could ask to be excused. Theirs were not discussions one saw on Downton Abbey where interjection came easy. Their discussions got quickly impassioned, making it hard to participate, let alone interject to ask for permission to leave.

So, while the adults were debating, I squeezed between my mother's chair and the wall and made my escape to the living room to pet my grandfather's dog, Laika, browse Readers Digests, or sit, waiting to hear them call me after they realized I had snuck out. Sometimes they were so engrossed in their discussions they didn't notice me sneak out the door. There were times a slight pause in the debates allowed me to ask permission and avoid getting in trouble, but most times I snuck out. Sometimes they didn't notice my escape for close to an hour. Then, I was called back in, made to sit in my chair, told I needed to be excused, and then, after having been given permission, was allowed to return to whatever I had been doing.

My grandfather even had strict rules for Laika, who was named for the Russian dog sent into space. When Laika was a puppy, my grandfather sent him for training. Laika was expected to be well be-haved and to follow rules, like laying on a particular rug to earn a treat. It was a bit funny that Laika, a Siberian husky, talked back to my grandfather. In the end, Laika did what my grandfather asked, all the while vocalizing his displeasure. I think Laika was the only living being who could talk back to my grandfather and get away with it. That's not to say there was no discourse between the adults, but con-versations were usually one sided, with my grandfather being the one who had the last word.

The relationship between my grandfather and my mother was volatile. It was not as bad as the relationship between my grandfa-ther and uncle. Toward the end of my grandfather's life, my uncle spent more time with my grandfather. I wasn't there for the multiple head butting between the two. When my grandfather, uncle, and mother were together, however, it was a powder keg. When it was just my grandfather and my mother, it wasn't a matter of whether there would be an argument, but how bad the argument would be. I don't like being around confrontations. Knowing there was always a chance of a bad one between my grandfather and mother made me dread visits to my grandfather's house.

There were times when the disagreements were small, more along the lines of a loud debate. Other times, it was more a clash of personalities that became arguments and ended with us leaving. One time our trip was very short because the two had an argument. I didn't know what their argument was about, but it was bad enough that we left before the chairs warmed up. They had other arguments that we'd left after, but the visits were longer. Growing up, I had no idea why their relationship was the way it was. I saw they loved each other, but they didn't seem to know how to communicate in a way that didn't eventually devolve into a disagreement.

Even through all the discussions and arguments, I never heard anything said indicating my grandfather harbored hatred against a group of people. I heard bigoted remarks, but they were more apro-pos to his generation's ideals born from ignorance, not hate. For ex-ample, I once heard an older gentleman from an assisted living home describe his neighbors down the street. He had turned to another resident and said, "There are some black people who live in that house on the corner. They are so clean."

I was taken aback by his comment but knew that given the era in which he grew up, in his mind he had paid them a compliment. Anything I ever heard from my grandfather was no worse than that comment. He never said anything untoward around me that would have raised my suspicions there may have been more to his words than mere generations of change. Nothing about my grandfather supported the level of hate I discovered of his time in Lithuania.

One would think with the arguments and dread I felt about visiting my grandfather, it would be difficult for me to feel love toward him. His anger, however, was directed at my mother or my uncle, whether my uncle was there or not. His irritation was never focused on me. His interactions with me were always caring. I felt uncomfortable around the building anger between my grandfather and mother, but I figured it was just the way they were. I didn't understand why my grandfather got so angry. His anger made more sense to me after his past's secrets were uncovered.

So, why did I feel love for my grandfather? Not being the focus of his anger doesn't explain it. Our interactions were ones of love. He did little things to make me feel special. He bought me gifts at random times. If he saw a necklace or a pin he thought I'd like, he bought it for me. Never expensive, just little trinkets he saw in the store. He didn't wait for my birthday or Christmas to give me gifts. He justified this by saying he might not be around. Seeing the gleam in his eyes when he gave me gifts, told me he loved to give me things. And I loved getting his special surprises.

My grandfather showed me I was special to him in other ways. At times my mother and I visited my grandfather. My father had something scheduled, and my brother was allowed to stay home. After I visited for a bit with my grandfather, my mother and grandfather started discussing matters that didn't interest me. So, my grandfather suggested I watch television in his bedroom. The first time he offered felt strange. His bedroom was basically off-limits, even though it was right across the hallway from the dining room door. My mother told me not to get into anything. My grandfather told her I'd be fine. The first time I was allowed to watch television in my grandfather's bedroom, I took extra care to not do anything that might revoke his invitation.

In my teenaged years, my grandfather resolutely desired me to participate in their table discussions. While I was more interested in adult topics, I often found the heated discussions hard to take. Their discussions were usually 'everyone for themselves'. When I was in my early teens, I recall lingering at the table for the discussion. My uncle had come for dinner that day. I challenged something my uncle said, and he verbally attacked me. My grandfather admonished him. I had never witnessed my grandfather do that, and I had seen and heard some heated disputes in that house. While I was not completely comfortable with being the cause of my uncle's reprimand, my grandfather defending me made me feel good. It told me my input mattered and my grandfather thought highly of it.

My grandfather was proud that I excelled in school and planned on studying engineering in college. He wanted to get me a special gift for my high school graduation. At the beginning of my senior year of high school, he asked me to follow him into the dining room. On the table was a box that contained a small refrigerator for my dorm room. Of course, he said he was giving it to me then because he might not be around when I graduated. I hugged and kissed him and thanked him for my gift. I didn't think much about his disclaimer as to the timing of his gift. I had heard the same disclaimer so many times before, it had become a running joke to me. It was part of receiving my grandfather's gifts.

After I got my driver's license and was able to drive myself to soccer games, I didn't visit my grandfather with my mother every weekend. I either played in or refereed those games. I went with my mother on the days my games were early, and I'd be home before my mother headed to my grandfather's. By that time, though, my uncle lived with my grandfather, and their quarrels worsened. My grandfather and uncle clashed—them living together increased the hostility. I also witnessed my uncle's impact on my mother. Each weekend visit grew more tense than the previous one. I eventually looked for and found reasons to bow out.

A week before my high school graduation, my grandfather was admitted into the hospital. He used an inhaler and had had emphysema for many years but, there was no indications his health would suddenly decline. My uncle didn't notify my mother right away, so by the time we got the news, my grandfather was in bad shape. A couple of days before graduation, my grandfather passed. When my mother told me, I went to my room and cried for a long time. I had lost a person whom I loved and who I knew loved me. I lost a person who had always made me feel special. I also felt guilty for not visiting him more the past few years. I was sad I missed opportunities to spend time with him.

They didn't hold a memorial service for my grandfather. He was cremated. We took a Coast Guard boat onto Lake Erie to spread his ashes, as he requested. We dropped some flowers on the spot and then headed back to shore. At the time, I didn't question why there wasn't any service. I had been to several funerals on my father's side of the family. There was always a service, a burial, and then a reception afterward. It was a time for mourners to gather in celebration of the deceased's life and to catch up with one another. My grandfather's passing had none of that. I wasn't aware of any friends he may have had. As far as I knew, he only had us, his extended family, but my uncle's children (my cousins) didn't join us on the boat to spread his ashes. Because I knew my grandfather didn't leave home in his later life, I wasn't that surprised by the lack of service or reception. I never questioned why he wanted us to spread his ashes in the lake.

After high school graduation, I headed to college for the next phase of my life. I did so without my grandfather, who had been a big part of my life up to that point.

Chapter 4 ~ Secrets

There are no secrets that time does not reveal. —Jean Racine

It seemed like everything prior to what I could remember was shrouded in secrecy. When I got older, I started to realize I knew little about my mother's informative years and her family's history. The stories I'd heard most often were those of being in displaced persons' camps (now known as internment or refugee camps) in Germany, and they came to the United States on a ship. Otherwise, informational tidbits popped up from time-to-time—information like my grandfather got a job as a millwright in America, even though he was a drafter in Lithuania. Most of the stories my mother told me were about her years as a teenager and even those weren't often shared. That may have been because my mother rebelled against my grandfather's rules and frequently skipped school. Not much about my mother's youth and her family's history before coming to the United States was discussed at my grandfather's house.

One of the few times I recall hearing about their lives in Lithuania was when my uncle discussed their escape. My uncle mentioned he remembered the Germans throwing grenades into house windows as he and his family left town. My uncle also relayed holding my mother's hand as they escaped through a field when she was only two. The only other stories I heard were from my mother, and those were about their time in the camp. Since she was a toddler when her family left Lithuania, she didn't remember much. Her memories ranged from vehement arguments between my grandparents, about them eating licorice root, and her being hit in the head by a metal swing. It was like their lives began only after coming to the United States. I thought the reluctance to share their past stories was because they had lost their home to the war and were forced to live in a camp for several years. It was a time they more than likely didn't care to remember.

When I grew older, I wondered why they decided to leave Lithuania by retreating with the Germans rather than to stay as the Russians advanced, however, I knew people living there had the choice of siding with either fascists or communists—not much of a choice.

Neither government was one most people would've wanted to choose since each had their own brutal way of keeping populations in control. I thought perhaps they retreated with the Germans because my grandparents thought the Germans would be defeated, and the chance of living in a free society was greater if they left Lithuania than if they stayed under communist rule.

After my grandfather and uncle passed away, I learned more information about my mother's family which raised more questions. While not a floodgate of stories about her childhood, there were few I'd not heard. She revealed information that, being the last remaining person in her family who made the move to the United States, I feel that she felt comfortable sharing.

The first reveal, while not one that led to our "big" family secret, was one that showed how unforthcoming my family was regarding their past as it wasn't something one needed to hide. My uncle was someone who came in and out of my life at different times. I felt he was an outsider to our family and the cause of a lot of strife. I presumed my grandfather and uncle conflicted because my uncle seemed irresponsible. After my aunt divorced him, he was homeless with a drinking problem for a time. That kind of behavior my grandfather would see as inappropriate. Emotions ran high when my uncle's situation was discussed.

I discovered there was more to my grandfather and uncle's tense relationship than my uncle's living situation and alcohol issues. Shortly after my uncle's memorial service, my mom revealed he was her half-brother and not my grandfather's son. I don't understand why that secret was held for so long or why it was a secret in the first place. It may have been because it made U.S. immigration paperwork easier not having to deal with a blended-family situation. Even though my uncle was a naturalized citizen, his secret was kept from the rest of our family until after he passed away.

I've not been told how old my uncle was when my grandparents married. I don't know how old my uncle was when his father was no longer in his life. My mother was told my grandmother had divorced my uncle's father, but my mother wasn't told why. I presume that not being my grandfather's son helped account for the distance between him and my grandfather and him being seen as an outsider.

My uncle's familial relationship to my grandfather and mother was not a secret (I thought) that should have been kept for so long. It is an example, however, of how much information was withheld from them prior to them coming to the United States. The limiting sharing of information impacted my mother's knowledge of her own family's history. My mother said she wished she could learn more about her family's Lithuanian history. Since my mother was a toddler when they left, she remembers little about her extended family or about living in Lithuania. She shared memories in bits and pieces that raised more questions for me.

It may have been due to my mother's family immigrating to the United States at the end of World War II or because WWII was a pivotal time in the world's history, but I found myself delving into what I could about the war. I watched programs on the History Channel and read books on it. I was interested in not only the progression of the war but also the interactions between the people involved. That included the ways in which the Nazis and Japanese interacted with the populations they conquered. Understanding how the conquered populations were viewed led to my initial questions about my grandfather's role in WWII.

My mother told me that when she was younger, she asked questions about life before the family left Lithuania, but her questions remained unanswered. She stopped asking because she felt her parents didn't want to talk about it and it was inappropriate to inquire. One of the things she told me she remembered was being told Nazi officers attended special occasions in their home. That caught my attention. I knew Nazi officers and locals of the captured areas didn't interact unless the locals were held in high regard by or were collaborating with the Nazis. It would be one thing for my grandfather to not resist the Nazi occupation and conduct himself to ensure his family survived, as many did during the war. It would be another to create a relationship with the Nazi officers to the point of them attending special family occasions like my mother's christening. That kind of relationship would involve going beyond survival tactics.

While questions grew regarding my grandfather's role in the Nazi occupation of Lithuania, I never fathomed the truth would be anything close to what I later discovered. Those questions were ones to which I needed to find answers. However, there was no one I could directly ask.

With my growing confusion, I felt the need to find information on my grandfather. I periodically did internet searches on his name and Lithuania. Since the sought records would've been prior to the end of World War II—and old Lithuanian records, if they survived the bombings, may not have been transferred to the internet, I wasn't finding any information. I found a Lithuanian genealogy page that searched for records, but the page stated it could take a year or more before anyone replied, so I never followed through. I'm unsure why I made that decision at the time. It may have been because I wasn't ready for the answers at the time, or perhaps I was waiting for other kinds of records to become available without the wait.

The next time my mother shared a story, it pointed toward a dark truth. I was visiting my parents' house in Texas Hill Country from Oklahoma. We were in their pool, chatting. I don't recall how the topic came up, but my mother shared an odd interaction she had with my grandfather. My father had read an article on a war criminal who was wanted and thought to reside in the Cleveland area. The person being sought came to the United States on the *USS Hershey*—the first refugee ship to come to the United States. My father asked my mother if the person being described sounded anything like my grandfather. The depiction raised my mother's suspicions enough, she called my grandfather. Instead of answering her questions on the phone, he asked for my parents to drive to his house so they could talk in person.

My parents made the thirty-minute drive. My mother told me my grandfather said he attended a small event that had happened. He told them he was there but did not participate and no one was killed. He basically told them he witnessed people being harassed and harmed. I don't know what my parents would've done had he admitted to participating in the harassment of Jewish people, but since he admitted to only being there, the subject was dropped.

Unlike with my parents, his story set off alarm bells for me. While my grandfather's story could've been accurate, I knew my grandfather wouldn't have admitted to being the person the article described. I became concerned about my grandfather's past and that my parents read the news article and thought the war criminal's description sounded like my grandfather. With the added information grandfather left Lithuania as the Germans retreated, combined with the lack of family history before coming to the United States, I questioned his story. I grew scared my grandfather may have been a Nazi collaborator, although I never imagined the level of his involvement I would discover.

I renewed my search on my grandfather's name, Anatolijus Dagys, and added search terms such as "Lithuania," "Holocaust," and "Nazi." One of my searches eventually pulled up an article by Arunas Bubnys on the Lithuanian Auxiliary Police. Bubnys had written his article on Lithuanian Auxiliary Police's role played in the Nazi's elimination of the Lithuanian Jewish populace.

When I read the article, I found several references to an A. Dagys, who was a lieutenant in one of the units. The name was associated with four different mass executions of Jewish people. With only a last name (relatively common in Lithuania), I knew there was a chance it was not my grandfather. But with the information I'd found, I needed to discern if my grandfather was the person the article referenced. I knew someone who was recorded as being involved in leading death squads and was highly revered by Nazis had a name like my grandfather. I had to follow the information to wherever it led.

I ran into a problem when I attempted to track down the author's contact information. A person at the organization that published the article gave me the author's contact information but informed me I'd have to converse with him in German. The problem was I couldn't speak German, but a former coworker was from Germany. It took me a while to decide to enlist her help in translating an email to the author. To do so, I had to explain a little about why I needed her help, which was not easy. Fortunately—or unfortunately—due to the information the communication would afford me, she was willing to help me communicate with the article's author.

This is the email I sent to the author:

Hello Dr. Bubnys,

My name is Kerrie Taber. My grandfather is Anatol (Anatolijus) Dagys. A little over a year ago, my mother told me a story about an article that was in a newspaper many years ago that described a wanted war criminal. This description sounded like my grandfather, so she went to question him. She told me that when she questioned him about the article, he admitted that he participated in one incident during the war. It did not seem to fit that there would be an article if he only participated in one incident. She also said that she had been told that German officers attended her christening, which seemed to point to more than a brief interaction with the Nazis. I have been searching the web off and on for the past year to try to find out more information about the connections between Lithuanians and the German occupation. I have also been looking for possible information about my grandfather. Just recently, I found your paper *Lithuanian Police Battalions and the Holocaust (1941-1943)*. In the article, there is a Liet. A. Dagys mentioned in the descriptions of the activities of the 1st Battalion 3rd Company. I obtained your email from the Secretariat of the International Commission for the Evaluation of the Crimes of the Nazi and Soviet Occupation Regimes in Lithuania. I am writing you with the hope that either you can confirm if this is or is not Anatolijus Dagys.

What I read in your paper does not fit with the man I knew as my grandfather, but I know that I knew him at a different time in a different place. I am searching for this information because I just feel the need to know what is hidden in my family's past, whether that is good or bad.

I appreciate any help you can give me.

Best Regards,

Kerrie Taber

I got a reply in less than a day.

Dear Kerrie Taber,

I can give you some information about Anatolijus Dagys (born on 22 October 1909 in Russia). Before the Nazi-Soviet War in 1941, he served in the Red Army in the 215th regiment. On July 3, 1941, Dagys was in the Lithuanian Auxiliary Police Battalion (in Lithuanian Tautos Darbo Apsaugos Batalionas, TDA) in Kaunas as deputy leader of the 3rd company. This battalion (especially the 3rd company) was involved in many mass murders of Jews in Kaunas and other places in Lithuania in the summer and autumn of 1941. According to my research, this battalion together with German SS members murdered no less than 39,000 Jews. On August 25, 1941, Lieutenant A. Dagys became the leader of the 3rd company of the battalion. During the whole period, A. Dagys served in the Lithuanian police battalions during the Nazi occupation in Lithuania. After the war, A. Dagys lived in the USA. His wife's name was Ona Apsegaite (Kuzmiene).

All the best,

Dr. Aruna Bubnys

The information in Bubnys' email was such that there was no denying his article referred to my grandfather. The saying, "don't ask the question if you don't want the answer" came to mind. The man I loved. The man who treated me special. The man I thought I knew was a mass murderer. He led men who shot men, women, and children. He did more than just "happen to witness" an event where "something" had happened. He participated in and ordered others to participate in the killings of tens of thousands of innocent people. Reading the accounts of my grandfather's actions and those his unit took in assisting Nazis was not easy. Even if he was involved with killing one innocent person, it would be one too many and was hard to reconcile with the person I knew. Trying to fathom my grandfather being in a battalion involved in the deaths of tens of thousands of men, women, and children was incomprehensible, however, there was no denying the facts.

Chapter 5 ~ The Brutal Truth

Three things cannot be hidden: the sun, the moon, and then truth. —Buddha

Although I had a hard time accepting the man in Dr. Bubnys' article was my grandfather, what I thought I would find was my grandfather was no more than a guard, a crime for which many other non-Germans were arrested. I didn't consider his role was much more involved and much harder to reconcile. That man who treated me special was stated as being highly regarded by the Nazis and was implicated in genocide. It's one thing to read about the Holocaust and the mass killings in the camps via gas chambers. It's quite another to read about the execution of men, women, and children in small groups by firing squads combined with the horror of realizing your loved one was associated with those murders.

Most of the Holocaust focus has been on the Polish concentration camps. Little has been discussed about the implementation of genocide in other camps. In Lithuania, the Jews were not sent away after being placed in ghettos. The Lithuanian Auxiliary Police, particularly the flying squads, were tasked to empty the ghettos under the direction of the German Special Unit (Waffenschutzstaffel-SS). In the Kaunas area, where my grandfather lived, the Lithuanian Auxiliary Police "cleansed" the area of nearly all Jews.

Kaunas was the center of Eastern Europe's Jewish community with approximately one hundred Jewish organizations, forty synagogues, five daily newspapers, schools for all ages, and a teachers' college. Approximately 40,000 Jews, about a quarter of the city's population, lived in the area when the Germans invaded. Prior to that, the Lithuanians revolted against the Soviets in the hopes they could remain an independent country under German rule. During that time, several local citizens harassed and killed Jews. In addition to antisemitism, the non-Jewish population had an aversion toward Jewish people's support of the Soviet rule for taking leadership positions in the Soviet-backed government. Thousands of Jews were assaulted or killed between the time Lithuania gained Soviet independence and the German occupation in June 1941.

In one case, fifty Jewish men were attacked and killed by a crowd at Kaunas' Lietukis Garage. The crowd struck the men, hosed them, and then beat them to death with metal bars. The horror was documented with photos showing men lying face down in the mud while others viewed the bodies.

The photos brought to my mind the lynching from America's southern history. I wondered if my grandfather was referring to the garage event when he denied any participation after my parents' confrontation. The photos show many people, many of whom are in uniform, standing around the victims, which adds to my suspicion one of them was my grandfather. Chances are, many in the crowd watched but did not participate. I haven't found any documentation naming participants in the killings, so there's no way for me to know for sure. Given the information I found, however, I have a strong suspicion he was one of the perpetrators in those killings.

Nazis wasted no time "cleansing" Lithuania of Jews. After they documented the Jewish population by age and gender, the Nazis began eliminating Jews in areas around Lithuania. The German Security Police (SD) and the SS, who were tasked with Jewish extermination, weren't able to complete that task on their own, particularly in Kaunas County. They requested assistance from the National Labour Defense Battalion (TDA), better known as the Lithuanian Auxiliary Police.

The Lithuanian Auxiliary Police was formed to end resistance to the German occupation. After the resistance was put down, the police force then implemented the area's execution of Jews. At that time, 3rd Company, 1st Battalion combined forces with the Nazis to massacre Lithuanian Jews. 3rd Company, 1st Battalion, where my grandfather was a lieutenant, was known as part of the flying squads that came into an area after the Jews were gathered to conduct the executions. The 3rd company of the 1st battalion was often the unit the Nazis called upon to perform executions and was made up of specially chosen men.

The executions were unlike the concentration camp executions most people learn about. There were no gas chambers, or their predecessors—delivery trucks with the condemned locked inside and the exhaust fumes piped into the back. The executions were personal. The Jews were lined up next to a trench and were shot in the head. The Nazis eventually used trucks and gas chambers because shooting Jews took a mental toll on soldiers. The murders apparently didn't have any impact on my grandfather as he was listed in official German and eyewitness reports as taking part in at least five mass-shooting executions.

My grandfather was associated with several mass murders through the official reports, three of which stated he was in charge of the unit which traveled to surrounding villages and executed detainees. Two of the events that my grandfather is recorded as taking part in took place within Kaunas and involved the killing of thousands of Jewish people. To accommodate large number of Jewish people, some of the old forts were used as the initial holding areas and then the location of the executions. The Seventh Fort was the first one used, but the Ninth Fort will become the main location in Kaunas for many executions of Jewish people from Lithuania and other places around Europe.

While Kaunas County's Jewish population elimination took only a few months, the executed numbered in the tens of thousands. After all the Kaunas County Jews were exterminated, Jews were transferred from other European areas to Kaunas County, particularly to the area's forts, to be executed.

The Kaunas County massacres committed by my grandfather's battalion occurred between July 4th to the end of October 1941. When all told, the total of Jewish murders with which my grandfather was associated, numbered over ten thousand.

The Seventh Fort was the first major mass execution of Jewish people and was the first recorded event my grandfather took part in. The killings would go on for two days. The 1st Battalion played a leading role in the killings, with my grandfather being prominently mentioned in the official German reports and those from eyewitnesses.

The Jews were marched from the ghetto across the river to the Seventh Fort. The nights prior to their deaths, the men slept outside in a ravine, and the women were held in an underground area. There were 416 men and 47 women sleeping their last night alive at the fort.

When the executions started on July 4th, the guards took ten people from the group and led them to a crater that had been formed by an explosion. The Jews were lined up along the edge with their backs to the soldiers. The soldiers aimed their rifles. The officers, like my grandfather, aimed their pistols. The officer gave the order, and they all fired. The dead bodies fell into the crater, and the next group of ten were led to the crater's edge. The process was repeated until dark.

The following day, soldiers surrounded the ravine where remaining male Jews slept. Instead of moving the men to the crater, soldiers fired their weapons, including machine guns, into the ravine. Due to the depth of the ravine, the detained men were not able to escape. The onslaught lasted about an hour and a half. Dead bodies and blood filled the ravine. The ravine killings' official report noted two 1st Battalion lieutenants but not my grandfather. It's impossible to know if he was a witness of or participant in the ravine murders. Regardless, he would've been fully aware of the massacre.

On July 6th, more Jews were moved into the Seventh Fort. To help expedite the massacre, machine guns were once again used. Larger groups were lined up and shot. Some witnesses stated that when a new group arrived at the crater, they were made to cover the previous victims with dirt and calcium oxide (lime) to reduce the smell the corpses would eventually emit. My grandfather took part in that day's massacre of 2,514 Jews.

At the end of the three days, around 5,000 to 8,000 Jews—men and women—either lay dead in the crater or in the ravine.

In later interviews, soldiers who participated in the slaughter noted some of their comrades suddenly wanted to only guard the detained Jews and refused rotation to the firing squads—they could not continue shooting people. By July 11th, one-hundred-and-seventeen men had been discharged, one company commander committed suicide, and many others simply deserted. Those men found it difficult to shoot a person in the back. That apparently was not the case with my grandfather. A month after shooting thousands in the Seventh Fort, my grandfather led other mass executions in surrounding towns and participated in at least one other massacre at a Kaunas fort.

Many of the future executions occurred at villages around Kaunas. Prior to the flying squads' arrival, the local partisans transferred the area Jews to one location. In most of the remote locations, the Nazis followed a specific protocol. Once the Jews were gathered, Nazi officers travelled to pick a location for the executions. Then, in preparation, local or detained male Jews dug trenches. Once the Jews had been confined and the trenches were ready, the town notified the Nazis it was ready for the flying squad.

After the Seventh Fort, the next location my grandfather, along with Lieutenant Paulikonison, led executions was in the Petrašiūnai area, located on Kaunas' eastern side. Those executions were conducted at the end of August 1941. When commanded, my grandfather arrived in one of two trucks from the 1st Battalion carrying approximately forty men. Small groups of the condemned were led by the local partisans, who acted as guards to one of the two trenches, and were lined up along the edge with their backs to their executioners. My grandfather and the other lieutenant gave the firing orders. When the people were shot dead, guards led the next group to the trenches. The process continued until all victims had been shot. When the executions were completed, 125 Jews—thirty men, seventy-two women, and twenty-three children—lie dead or dying in the trenches. After the last Jew was killed, the executioners climbed into their trucks. Their job completed, it was time to head home to their barracks and families.

Also, at the end of August, my grandfather led the 1st Battalion into Garliava, to the south of Kaunas. The Jews had been gathered in the synagogue by the local police and partisans. Synagogues were often used as Jewish ghettos or holding centers in preparation for the executions. When the execution date approached, local police and partisans brought a few men to the execution site. They told the detainees to dig trenches under the pretense of releasing water. The men refused, however, when they realized the truth. Once the Jews refused to dig their own mass grave, the police were forced to make locals dig them.

When the 1st Battalion arrived, the Jews were forced to walk to their execution site. The condemned were stopped out of sight of the trenches but remained close enough. As with previous executions, Jews in smaller groups were then lined up and shot in the back. Since executions started late in the afternoon, they weren't completed until nightfall. Soldiers lit the area with torches and stayed to finish off the injured. By the end of the night, the trench was filled with 249 Jews—seventy-three men, one-hundred-and-thirteen women, and sixty-three children.

After shooting the Jews, the soldiers headed to the town's pub and drank beer with the locals before heading home. While the soldiers, my grandfather, and local men who assisted in the killings drank, the still-warm bodies of 249 people lied nearby in freshly covered pit. Going to a pub after killing even one person, much less multiple people whose only crime was being Jewish, is incomprehensible to me. It seems as if my grandfather and the other participants saw the massacre as just another day at work. What's more natural than heading to the bar with your coworkers after work? But when combined with the genocide those men committed, gathering for an after-work drink made the killers appear even more callous.

At the beginning of September, my grandfather took part in the executions in the town of Babtai. That location held a combination of Babtai and Vandžiogala Jews. They were also held in the local synagogue while they awaited their fate. A trench was dug in the forest near the river and was completed in the early afternoon. The Nazi sympathizers forced the Jews to walk from the synagogue to the trench. Those who could not walk very well—the old and very young—were taken by carriages to the location. That time, the executions were done in a particular order. The prisoners were forced to disrobe down to their underwear. The executioners started with the men and then moved on to the women. Once the men and women's bodies lied in the trench dead or dying, the children were taken to the trench.

The unimaginable scene that must have taken place when after the children, who witnessed their parents being led away and heard gunshots, then stood along the trench's edge that contained the adult's bodies, including their parents. As the shooting continued, the following young victims would have seen other children's bodies in the trench.

After the children were dispatched, those who were unable to walk were taken by carriages to the trench. They were thrown into the trench with their dead companions and shot.

It took several hours for the soldiers to execute the approximate 335 Jews. When they were finished, the locals and the soldiers sifted through the victim's belongings for anything of value. When done rummaging, the soldiers loaded into their vehicles and went home.

In October, the massacres moved to Kaunas' Ninth Fort. By having the executions at the Ninth Fort, which was located two kilometers outside the city, it was easier to keep the executions private. Privacy was a problem in early July with Seventh Fort's executions, which happened within the city limits. The largest number of executions throughout the German occupation of Lithuania transpired in Kaunas' Ninth Fort. An estimated 40,000 people were executed there between October 1941 and the spring of 1944, when the advancing Soviets pushed Germans out of Lithuania and ended the mass killing of Jewish people in the country.

On October 29, 1941, the largest single mass murder of Lithuanian Jews occurred.

The Kaunas ghetto had been filled with Jews from around Lithuania. The selected Jews from the ghetto were taken to the Ninth Fort. According to an account from a 1st Battalion soldier, on the night of the 28th, either my grandfather or another lieutenant told the soldiers not to drink alcohol and to be ready early the following morning. Due to the number of Jews to be executed, the entire battalion was involved. One leg of the battalion transferred approximately 400 Jews from the ghetto to the Ninth Fort. Another leg guarded and moved the Jews to their execution spot. The first group of soldiers then headed back to the ghetto for more Jews.

Three large trenches were dug behind the fort. The last group of soldiers, which included my grandfather, were positioned at that location. The soldiers commanded their prisoners to strip, and then led small groups to the trenches. The soldiers lined up the prisoners along trenches and shot them in their backs. As with other massacres at the Kaunas' forts around, witnesses stated the next group to be executed were made to cover the previous victims with dirt and calcium oxide. German soldiers armed with automatic weapons participated in the massacre alongside the 1st Battalion. That was a unique instance as German troops rarely participated in the Kaunas massacres. No records exist as to why the Germans took a more active role in that event. In other area massacres, the German soldiers' roles mainly were determining the trench locations and ordering the flying squad to the site.

The process of moving the condemned people from the ghetto to the Ninth Fort and then to the trenches continued all day until

47

9,200 Jews—2,007 men, 2,920 women, and 4,273 children—filled the Ninth Fort trenches.

My grandfather was mentioned by name in an official German report on October 29, 1941—the date of the last massacre. Between July 4th and October 29th encompasses the dates of documented killings associated with my grandfather. My grandfather participated in the murder of at least 14,000 Jewish men, women, and children. Historians have made strong speculations that the 3rd company of the 1st Battalion participated in many other massacres. If their speculations are correct, the unit could have been involved in tens of thousands more Jews' deaths.

SS Colonel Karl Jager, the Nazi commander in charge of eliminating people of Jewish descent, reported in December 1941 that, *"Today I can confirm that Strike Commando 3 has reached the goal of solving the Jewish problem in Lithuania. The only remaining Jews are laborers and their families."*

Of those who remained, Colonel Jager stated, *"I am of the opinion that the male work Jews should be sterilized immediately to prevent any procreation. A Jewess who nevertheless becomes pregnant is to be liquidated."*

While the Jews were essentially wiped out in Lithuania, massacres continued as soldiers brought in Jews from all over Europe into Lithuania. While my grandfather was not mentioned by name in any published document as a participant after October 29, 1941, the 1st Battalion was known to have been part of the continued mass murders. Chances are my grandfather was involved in some capacity with additional Ninth Fort killings.

While I would like to believe my grandfather chose to stop participating in the slaughters, I don't think that's the case, my mother, who was born in 1942, mentioned that Nazis attended her christening. That indicated a good relationship between my grandfather and the Nazis even after October 29, 1941. Documentation exists which indicated my grandfather was moved into a more administrative role. The exact timing for the transition is unknown. By October, no people of Jewish descent lived outside the Kaunas ghetto, and in the ghetto, their numbers were small.

The number of people my grandfather's unit and company killed overall is hard for me to comprehend. Tens of thousands of people taken in small groups, lined up along a trench or crater, and then were shot in the back. Those people most likely would have had a strong suspicion as to their fates even before the soldiers took the first group. After the first group, they would've heard gunshots, confirming their fears. Then, when subsequent groups arrived at the execution site, they would've looked into the trench. They would've seen bodies of dead and dying people. They would have known their short futures held the same fate.

While the act of killing is hard for me to conceive, when I cogitated what my grandfather did to the children repulsed me. Most people have an instinct to protect children from harm, regardless of relationship. Instead, my grandfather ordered and directly participated in murdering children. After he finished, he went home to his family—which until 1942, included my grandmother and my then eight-year-old uncle. After wiping out entire families, my grandfather evidently went home to his as if he had not just executed genocide, an act considered reprehensible in every civilized society. After learning of my grandfather's active role in WWII, in my heart he went from a man I loved to a horrendous monster whose unspeakable deeds went against everything I was taught and believed in.

Chapter 6 ~ Through a Different Lens and Coming to Terms

Truth will always be truth, regardless of lack of understanding, disbelief, or ignorance. —W. Clement Stone

Revelations about my grandfather's past put new meanings to his words and actions. Especially if had he been found by Nazi-sympathizer hunters. He would have been extradited to Lithuania to be hung, which was the fate of at least two of the lieutenants he served with. The pressure had to have caused high levels of stress and paranoia. I can't imagine living almost forty years in fear of someone knocking at my door to be held accountable and executed in Lithuania. Even so, I have no sympathy for my grandfather or how stress and paranoia may have had an impact on him living his life.

Learning about my grandfather's past changed the way I viewed him. The information I learned also answered questions I'd had about decisions my grandfather made. I had often wondered why my grandparents immigrated to Germany instead of staying in Lithuania. I thought they picked the lesser of two evils. As the Germans retreated, my grandparents chose between staying under Soviet rule, or relocate to Germany and under fascist control, even though the German military showed signs of collapse. With new information, their reasons became clear. Had they stayed, my grandparents likely would have been killed. Who knows what would have become of my uncle and mother?

The crumbling of the Nazi regime and the following arrests of those who assisted in the Final Solution would have been a difficult time for my grandfather's family as they waited in the internment camp. My grandparents descended from the top of society. My grandfather controlled life and death and was held in high esteem by the Nazi government one moment, and the next lived impoverished and anonymous in a camp. Those camps were often in areas that had been bombed during the war, and several families were housed in one area of a building.

A person might wonder how my grandfather was able to avoid detection and allowed to immigrate to the United States with his family considering his active role in the Holocaust. Several factors prevented their detection. First, while Germans were known for their record keeping, those records were not kept the way they are today, which are in searchable databases. Also, my grandfather's deeds were concentrated in Lithuania, which was under Soviet control. The Soviets didn't assist the British and Americans with hunting down fugitive war criminals. Other Lithuanians who chose to escape to Germany also likely collaborated with the German soldiers. Doubtful the deserters would notify authorities about my grandfather as they possibly were avoiding arrest. Add to those reasons the chaos prevalent after the end of World War II.

The CIA supplied paperwork to hand-picked Holocaust perpetrators which allowed them to immigrate to the United States. While this may not have been the case for my grandfather, the United States government overlooked those people's Nazi involvement as they could potentially identify Soviet spies. My grandfather and his family spent six years in the displaced persons camps before paperwork was ready for them to take the *USS Hershey* to the United States. Six years of my grandfather hoping no one would identify him as the murderer of thousands of people, and six years of harsh reminders of how far he had fallen in society.

The stress of convincing authorities to allow my grandfather's family to immigrate to the United States, while hoping his role in Lithuania would not be discovered, added to the stresses of living in cramped quarters, probably made life challenging. Based on my observations of my grandfather's personality added to the stresses of their living situation, the story of my grandmother pulling a knife on him during one of their arguments made more sense. I have no way of knowing if violent arguments between my grandparents were typical or if that incident was a symptom of their situation. I don't recall any other accounts of domestic violence. I have no memory of my grandmother or her overall personality as she passed away when I was around two years old. Their world had crumbled, and the fear of being discovered before they could emigrate from Europe may have been overwhelming. The stress of their situation and the resentment of their social decline might have elevated, cutting fuses short.

As I reflected on decisions and actions my grandparents made in light of my new-found knowledge, additional questions and new understandings took shape. That was especially true when I realized how much my grandfather's ability to hide his identity meant to maintaining his lifestyle. My grandparents only allowing English to be spoken in the house was one of his decisions. I thought my grandfather had made that decision to better fit in their new country. While that was true at the time for many immigrants and may have played a part, stopping all Lithuanian communications and customs was one way he hid his past. Other than private family holiday meals and various knickknacks, there were no signs of our Lithuanian background in his home. With how little it was mentioned, it was if my grandfather, not my mother, was the child immigrant to the United States. It became apparent to me, my grandfather's decision to remove Lithuanian was made to distance him from his past.

To make a living, my grandfather worked as a millwright. One would be hard-pressed to discern if my grandfather's demotion was part of his attempt to hide or if his drafting degree/experience was unrecognized in the United States, which was a problem for degreed immigrants who didn't earn their education or experience here. Additionally, any drafting-related records remained in Lithuania behind the Iron Curtain and out of my grandfather's reach. Any attempt to obtain copies would have disclosed his whereabouts. Either way, he went from being a drafter and a highly regarded lieutenant to a janitor. That most likely added to my grandparents' stress and may have acted as a continual reminder of how far they had fallen from grace. Working at a menial task that often goes unnoticed was a good place for an execution squad's leader to hide in plain sight.

Direct experiences with my grandfather started to take on new meanings. For example, when my grandfather gave me gifts and said he may not be around for the upcoming occasions, now makes sense. I thought he was being fatalistic and thought he would die before the event. The United States created the Office of Special Investigations under the Justice Department to hunt down Nazi war criminals, in 1979. They quickly caught several sought-after war criminals. Had my grandfather's secret been uncovered and with his knowledge of that organization, I think he said that to me because he feared he could be arrested at any time.

Even after over twenty years, my grandfather probably felt he would be found. The organization and the arrests of war criminals years after their crimes may have made him feel his luck was running out. My grandfather would have seen news on the arrests, citizenships revocations, and the trials of the war criminals. One arrest that should have hit close to home was of John Demjanjuk in 1979, in a city ten miles from where my grandfather lived. After many years of citizenship-revocation trials, Demjanjuk was convicted in 1988 of being an accessory to murder in the deaths of 28,000 victims in Sobibor. The trial and conviction made national news but was particularly big news in Cleveland. Every day, my grandfather would have seen newspaper articles and news stories on the television about Demjanjuk. Stories about war criminals being arrested and that particular one (due to geographical proximity) would have been a stark reminder of how fleeting his freedom was.

The fortress my grandfather created around his house and his reluctance to leave it took on a different feel. Even though bushes surrounded the front yard and the sides of the backyard, and the lilac bush blocked one end of the porch, his window sheers were continuously drawn. While those devices might not have kept people out, the idea his house was hidden from the outside world most likely gave my grandfather a sense of security. That sense of security probably limited his excursions to running necessary errands. The thirty-minute trip to our house in Elyria most likely made him uncomfortable. He would have been far away from his safe zone where he hid from the people who hunted him. Traveling to our house increased the chances of being pulled over or an unforeseen occurrence, such as an accident, which would involve the police. His homebound desires made the excursion to watch me play soccer mean even more and explains why he left early.

Most of the time I knew my grandfather was after the creation of the Office of Special Investigations and the Simon Wiesenthal Center, a Jewish organization that also hunted Nazis. I don't know if his aggressive personality was who he was or due to stress from fear of being caught. I know from my mother's stories he'd been a strict parent. Again, it's hard to know if he was that way before the war or if that came about after. It's also hard to know if my grandfather, uncle, and mother behaved in certain ways because they were uprooted from their home and spent years in a camp awaiting emigration papers, and if any of their behaviors were impacted by my grandfather's fear of being arrested.

It's obvious to me now my mother's unstable childhood mentally impacted her behaviors. My mother recently relayed a story to me about why she cuts the vegetables so small for potato salad. She had once prepared it for a holiday meal. My grandfather informed her she hadn't cut the pieces small enough. To this day, my mother cuts vegetables into very small pieces. She told me she doesn't know why something my grandfather said decades ago causes her to dice them that way to this day. While my mother and I harbor none of my grandfather's hate, the impacts of his behaviors are felt in myriad ways.

The emotional and mental impacts grandfather caused held power long after his death. When I first read Bubnys' article, I was confused, angry, disappointed, saddened, and lost. I couldn't understand how the man I loved so much and thought I knew could do something so heinous—that the man who treated me so special could point a pistol at a child, a little girl who may have been much like me and pull the trigger. Some people question how a person hadn't an inkling their neighbor was a monster, much less that their family member was one. Several serial killers went undetected for years. Some still roam free. An example of is the former was the BTK Killer. Dennis Rader, known to many as a respected family man and a church leader, killed at least ten people over seventeen years. Serial killers often live two separate lives that allow them to hide their dark secrets. When I discovered I had lived intimately close to a monster, my grandfather, I questioned my perceptions of others and clearly demonstrated to me how monsters hide in plain sight.

Even before I found out the truth about my grandfather, I sometimes wondered about the families of those associated with or arrested for heinous crimes. I wondered how they felt on learning the truth about the person they thought they knew so well. People outside the family question whether family members knew more than they wanted to admit. While that thought may be true in some cases, it does seem possible to not know someone's dark side, especially in one loved and admired. Articles and books written by and of family members mention the confusion and trauma experienced from learning the truth.

After I read the article about my grandfather, I felt I lost him all over again, but in a different way. I not only lost my grandfather when he passed away, I lost the good memories I had of him. From that point on, all my memories of him were tarnished. Any time I thought of him after I learned the truth, I imagined the man he was in

Lithuania, not the man I knew growing up. I no longer saw the man I grew up loving. I saw someone I wanted nothing to do with. I saw a stranger that I would have wanted to see extradited to Lithuania to receive punishment he deserved.

I understand how families of serial killers may have felt when the awful truth was exposed. I understand the denial family members of those arrested for war crimes stated in news articles. When discovering that a monster lives close by, people may find it easier to believe the stories are wrong. It's easier to believe it's a case of mistaken identity. In my case, it was harder to deny the information in the article. It was not a case of eyewitnesses identifying a person decades later or trying to match up an old fuzzy photo to a person who has significantly aged. It was an article based on German officers' reports that included names of those personally involved in the crimes. While I found information based on eyewitness reports, the information was in line with official German reports. It was much harder to claim my grandfather was a victim of mistaken identity when the name in the reports and the birthdate supplied by Bubnys left no doubt the articles spoke about my grandfather.

I regretted being curious and wanting to put pieces I knew about my mother's family together. Following the clues to the truth led me to something no one would want to know about a beloved family member. Once I had the information in my head, however, it was impossible to delete it from my brain. I knew the deep, heinous secret of my mother's father—a secret that hurt me to the very core of my being. How divergent my grandfather's actions were from who I am and what I believe.

I also had another dilemma—I was the only person in my family who knew the secret my grandfather probably thought died with him. Because my mother was so young when they left Lithuania, coupled with the way my grandfather hid, I don't think she ever knew the truth. I knew their relationship was a rocky one and did not want to take away what good feelings she may have had about her father. So, I kept my findings a secret from her and my family.

I used my family history in a diversity class I taught as an example that hate does not have to be passed on. I used my grandfather as an example when talking to friends about hate and terrorism. But I could not bring myself to share my findings with my family. How do you tell your mother that her father was a mass murderer and that some of the people he murdered were babies and children? How to do that when you have a hard time coming to terms with the knowledge yourself?

Whenever I told someone about my grandfather, I heard myself talking about it from an almost analytical position. It helped keep the pain I felt knowing who he was at bay. I told his story in the same way I recited a fact. It was no different than discussing any other aspect of history. I used it to support an idea. Deep down, maybe I thought that by seeing people's reactions to my family's dark secret, I confirmed I was not tarnished by him—that people would see I am not in any way a continuation of his hate.

For a while, I kept my pain buried deep. I guess one could say I used my family's talent of burying secrets and feelings to get on with life. It became more difficult when situations came up that reminded me of my grandfather. Though I tried to bury my pain and confusion deep inside me, like any dark secret, it ate away at me, even when I thought I was effectively handling the information.

What I was doing by burying my feelings and examining information from a fact-based viewpoint was allowing it to fester inside me. I carried my pain. I didn't release it and did not resolve the disparity I had between my grandfather's two lives. A trusted friend helped me work through the deception. I generally am not one who expresses feelings, so keeping them buried came natural for me. In hindsight, it may not have been the best thing for my mental health. Like my grandfather's past, my feelings were not going to stay hidden forever. During a discussion with my friend, I brought up what I found out about my grandfather. When I told my friend about my grandfather, the dam holding back the pain broke. I explained to my friend about how my grandfather made me feel loved and special. I spoke of what my grandfather had done in Lithuania. Through tears, I expressed all my feelings about my grandfather's past and how the truth impacted my memories of him.

It was the first time I felt I could openly talk about my grandfather and how the entire situation made me feel. We talked about my relationship with my grandfather and his history. We talked about my feelings of pain, confusion, and loss. My friend helped me see I could love my grandfather, but not the man he was in Lithuania. I could accept the way he made me feel without condoning his actions. My friend also said my grandfather's love towards me may have been his way of reconciling what he did. Through our discussions, I was able to hold on to the man I knew loved me while separating out the monster he was before I was born. I cannot say I feel the same way toward him as I did before I uncovered his secret, but I am able to hold on to some of that love without feeling supportive of his crimes. If he were still alive, I do not know if I could interact with him without seeing the monster. The separation of time between his death and my finding the truth about his history helps me hold on to some of the positive feelings I have for him.

Even after help regaining some of my love for my grandfather, I was having a hard time understanding how people could do what he and many other people did during the Holocaust and other genocidal events. Once I was able to develop a separation between the two sides of my grandfather, I did what came naturally when I was confused about something—I researched. I needed to understand how a person could participate in killing another. I needed to go beyond the simple explanation often given that people killed Jews because Hitler had said so. That reason for killing innocent, unarmed men, women, and children wasn't an adequate explanation. It failed to cover why so many people, the majority of which seemed like everyday people, hadn't any reservations about participating in mass murders. I needed information to help me come to terms with whom my grandfather was and the secrets he hid. I thought that by reading about Holocaust (and other genocidal events) participants, I would understand how there could be an inhumane side to my grandfather. My research took me to dark places of the human psyche, but it was a place I needed to be to help me understand my grandfather and others like him.

Chapter 7 ~ Making of Mass Murderers

When you think of the sort of things that happen when a genocide happens, it's again not people who are intrinsically evil. —Desmond Tutu

While it's difficult to fathom how a person could kill in cold blood, that they did it over and over again on a daily basis, every day, for months is incomprehensible. It was also difficult to reconcile my grandfather was one of those people. Yes, my grandfather was authoritative and controlling and was known to have a temper, but there was never an indication he killed so many people. Those who commit genocide go well beyond the actions of people in hate groups. Genocide deploys a systematic method to accomplish one goal: the destruction of a group of people. To understand the man I knew as my grandfather, I had to understand what caused men to mass murder people of Jewish descent, and how the killers could seamlessly blend into society. While my grandfather slaughtered in Lithuania, the origins of his orders to kill came from Nazi Germany.

Genocide is not limited to the Nazis and the Holocaust. While the Holocaust receives the most press, the twentieth century has been dubbed the "Age of Genocide." From 1904 until 1994, sixty million people have been victims of genocide. The Holocaust claimed approximately six million people of Jewish descent, or about two thirds of the European Jewish population in the 1940s. Three genocidal events occurred before the Holocaust. After the Holocaust which shocked the world, six cases of genocide occurred in the twentieth century. Sadly, the new millennium has not seen the end of genocide, as China is reportedly killing Uyghers, a Turkic ethnic group from northwestern China. In addition to genocide in China, ethnic-based killings have been occurring in other countries.

While the Holocaust was not the only genocide to occur in recent history, it is the most complex to explain due to the long-term, methodical, and controlled nature of the killings. The other aspect that makes it unique is it involved countless men, which made it more difficult to analyze. Many factors created an environment in which the Holocaust could occur.

One of the factors was antisemitism and general racism seen around the world. Prior to the Holocaust, Armenians were slaughtered in Turkey. From 1915-1917, between 600,000 to 1.5 million Armenians were killed by the Turks, and many others were expelled from the country, pushed into the desert, or forced to convert to Islam. The mass killings and violent actions against the Armenians elicited little response from outside countries. The lack of response may have emboldened Hitler to pursue genocide against the Jewish population.

In a meeting with his generals on August 22, 1939, Hitler informed his generals, *"Our war aim is not to attain a particular line [in the East], but the physical destruction of the enemy...who after all speaks today about the annihilation of the Armenians?"*

Countries seemingly shared a tacit agreement between them that each country could treat their citizens and operate within their own borders as they saw fit without interference.

The Nazi leadership studied how other countries handled racial engineering, ethnic mixing, and legal segregation. The Nazis sought to engineer effective racial order without visible evidence of extra-legal violence. After the war, reports and articles were found in the German Foreign Office, German Institute of Foreign Scholarship department on the discrimination of Blacks and Native Americans in the United States, laws against aboriginals in Australia, Scandinavia's sterilization laws, and Japanese views on race. The documents apparently were used as lessons and applied best practices toward a desired elimination of undesirables.

While other countries voiced concerns about the Nazi's treatment of the Jewish people, the Nazis claimed the U.S. lynching as a model condoning their actions and redirected focus off Germany. Julius Streicher, the editor of the German antisemitic newspaper *Der Stürmer* compared the anti-Jewish laws in place to lynching and stated calls for boycotts of the Olympics to be held in Germany were misplaced. His message to foreign countries was:

"People get excited abroad about the Kurfurstendamm affair, although as far as I know not a single Jew was killed. I would like to suggest to foreign countries that they should instead report about lynch justice in America. We pay no attention to Negro executions, so people

should not bother us when we lead racial offenders through the streets."

By shifting the world's focus to southern United States' lynching, the Nazis hoped to not only gain support for their institutionalized racism worldwide, but also from their own people, who would be asked to support laws that disenfranchised and removed the Jewish population from German society. In 1919, Hitler proclaimed he wanted antisemitism to be based in "facts" and not emotions to enable systemic disenfranchisement and removal of the Jewish people.

While antisemitism was not greater in Germany than in other European countries, it was the country where an antisemitic minority came into power. Using propaganda, political controls, and the emotional displays in Hitler's speeches, antisemitism was able to grow to the levels it did in less than a generation. The push of the government, a seed of moderate antisemitism, combined with easily proliferated lies, helped remove the supplied reality checks. The Great Depression made Germany fertile ground for genocide.

Hate is often grown toward a readily available scapegoat. In Germany's case, the moderate antisemitism supplied a target for the troubles Germany faced at the end of World War I. After the defeat, Germany was severely punished by the Allies through loss of land and (in today's equivalent) thirty-three billion dollars in reparations. Just over ten years after the war ended, the Great Depression hit, which further impacted an already struggling Germany.

While Germany had a history of blaming their Jewish population, the censure increased to a new level. A pamphlet, The German National Catechism, outlined reasons Jews were to blame for Germany's woes. The pamphlet incriminated Germany's defeat on Jewish treason. The accusation was that had the Jews not undermined the German military; Germany would have won the war. Additional reasons included: there were Jewish objectives to take over humanity, destroy works of culture, and conquer all other peoples. According to the pamphlet, the Jews would accomplish their goal by subjugating the world's population through control of money.

"How has the Jew dominated the peoples? With money. He lent them money and made them pay interest. Thousands and thousands of Germans have been made wretched by the Jews and been reduced to poverty. Farmers whose lands had been in the family for more than one

hundred years were driven from their lands because they could not pay the interest."

Due to the depression and economic impact of the war restitution, farmers struggled to make loan payments and lost their farms. The pamphlet writers supplemented the farmers' struggles, assigning responsibility to Jews.

The writers posited farmers:

"...[h]ad to move to the cities. Torn from the land to which they belonged, robbed of their labour that gave their lives purpose and meaning. They fell victim to poverty and misery. Worn down, their souls crushed, they accepted Jewish doctrines that denied the Fatherland and opposed all that was Nationalistic."

With the Great Depression combined with World War I recovery efforts and punishments instilled on Germany; the words fueled underlying antisemitism into accepted hate. The pamphlet and other propaganda like it made the "Plague of the Jews" Germany's main problem. Even though there wasn't any real conflict between German people and Jewish population prior to the rise of the Nazi party, derogatory remarks against the Jews may have been enough to instigate harm.

While the antisemitic propaganda and editorials helped create the "us vs. them" mentality, other factors helped make the German society vulnerable to the Nazis' ideals. Within the German population, there was a strong respect for authority. That respect made it harder for people to resist leader instigation and easier to foster an environment receptive to genocide.

The Nazis did not go straight from power to death camps. Steps were taken to dehumanize Jews and make actions against them acceptable. As German citizens bullied the Jews, Nazi politicians and judges did little to discourage their actions and were often viewed as encouraging the aggressions as release of pent-up frustrations caused by Jewish financial controls.

Self-defense and an ethical imperative were used as excuses for legal non-action and encouraging violence. German citizens began to consider destruction of Jewish property and violence against Jews as legal and obligatory. Due to the Jews' actions, German citizens believed they were being provoked into having to act. As individual acts of violence escalated, the Nazis didn't want to appear as unruly as lynchers, so they sought to put laws in place to stop "individual" actions. While in many cases the laws stopped the violence, the Germans created laws that codified crimes against the Jews.

The Nazis created the Nuremberg Laws to create "controlled" violence. That allowed violence to be seen as legal, as opposed to lynching, which was outside the law. The Nuremberg Laws, first enacted in 1935, were a series of laws put in place over several years revoking Jewish citizenship, segregating them from German society, limited their access to resources and livelihood, and justified violence. By removing Jewish people of their citizenship, the Germans also removed civil protections and legal resources. The laws essentially declared open season on German Jews.

While violence against Jews became a common occurrence, the most notorious occurred on November 9 and 10, 1938—a night that became known as Reichskristallnacht or the "Night of Broken Glass." Under Nazi encouragement and after a minor German diplomat was killed by a Jewish teenager, people in Germany and parts of Austria burned synagogues, beat Jews in the streets, and ransacked Jewish shops and homes. Police were told to step down and firemen were told not to respond to fires. By the end of the night, over a hundred Jews were killed and 30,000 Jews were arrested. Those arrested were sent to concentration camps. The removal of so many Jews shocked the Jewish community and caused fear about their future.

Nazi actions against the Jews took a more deadly turn when Germany invaded Soviet-controlled Poland on September 1, 1939. While the conditions in Germany were right for growth of antisemitism into violence, Poland perfectly fit Germany's plans for the Jews. While under Soviet control, many elites, those in government classes and nobles or landowners were executed. In their place, Ukrainians, Belarusians, and local Jewish communists took leadership roles in the government, education, and civic institutions. That not only made Jews appear to be Soviet allies, but also made them enemies of the Polish people. The Jews in that part of Poland were mainly orthodox and Hasidic, eastern Jews. Orthodox and Hasidic Jews were held in particular contempt. Jews who supported the Soviet occupation became a more vulnerable target of the Nazis and Poles who opposed the Soviet invasion. At that time the Nazis took steps to answer the "Jewish Question" to much harsher levels. With the invasion of

Poland, the Nazis created ghettos and concentration camps, which would be places of death for many Jews.

The ghettos helped provide material to Josef Goebbels, Nazi Propaganda Minister, to show Jews were subhuman. After being shown pictures of the Warsaw ghetto where Jews lived in filthy disease-ridden conditions, Goebbels declared, *"The Jews must be eliminated."*

Later, he visited the Lodz ghetto where he stated, *"These are no longer people, they are animals. This is therefore not a humanitarian but a surgical task. One must make incisions, extremely radical ones."*

Essentially, the Nazis used the ghetto's conditions, which they created by packing many people into an area with few or no resources, to justify the elimination through concentration camps.

As the Nazis continued their invasion to the east, Hitler issued the Commissars' Order. The order initially gave the SS permission to kill political leaders of the Red Army, who were often of Jewish descent. The order was later broadened to encompass all Jews in conquered territory. As the Nazis marched, they spread hate to fuel underlying antisemitism and recruited locals to help eliminate Jews. Jews, as in Poland, took administrative positions in areas under the Soviet control. That added to antisemitism that made Jews a target of anger and violence.

The spread of antisemitism into Lithuania found people who focused their ire on those who assisted the Soviets during the Soviet invasion. Once the Soviet army retreated, collaborators, regardless of their nationality, were attacked by Lithuanians who opposed the Soviet occupation. While non-Jews were attacked, the focus of their violence became Jews. Since Jews were being murdered prior to Nazi occupation of Lithuania, the Nazis found plenty of men, like my grandfather, willing to help the Germans rid the country of Jews. There was little need of propaganda to gain support for genocide. In fact, the time between Nazi control and the creation of the extermination units was relatively short.

While Jews had been murdered since the beginning of the Nazi regime, it was not until the Wannsee Conference in January 1942 where the "Final Solution" was produced. Prior to the conference, Hitler hadn't given an order to kill Jews. He hinted at the aspiration toward the end of 1941. Food shortages led Nazi officials to expedite eliminating Jews and other "useless eaters". While no one was ordered to eliminate the Jewish population, those who did were supported through promotions. The Wannsee Conference, attended by Reinhard Heydrich and Adolf Eichmann, created what became known as the "Final Solution"—the plan to transport Jews to death camps and gas chambers.

Escalation to the declaration of the "Final Solution" would not have been possible without the German people's support, who were perpetrators of violence. The number of people who actively or passively supported the violence was what made the Holocaust unique in terms of genocide. It was not a small subset of society. It was society as a whole who supported the escalating violence and segregation. The German people became accustomed to Jewish discrimination and cruelty from incidents of street vandalism and brutality They silently witnessed Jews' expulsion to concentration camps. As the violence escalated, social norms appeared to support victimization by allowing the creation of new laws.

The Nazi regime fueled the hate-led violence and tolerance of Jewish elimination—the public facilitated the Nazi vision. Individuals who lived apparently ordinary lives became active or passive participants in the deaths of six million Jewish citizens. Consensus was perpetrators of violence and death were unique in that they had a propensity for brutality. Many of the culprits of the Holocaust, however, were average. The transformation from ordinary folk to silent spectators of carnage or assassins was not unique to the Holocaust. The number of people who participated (either actively or passively) is. Throughout history, mass murders, genocides, and war crimes are often committed by average people, not degenerates. They were neighbors whose livelihoods rarely depend on the military or government.

Studies into German Reserve Police Battalion 101 revealed how seemingly ordinary people became participants in genocide. Browning and Goldhagan explored the organization and determined how the German people became complicit. Browning saw the killers as "ordinary people" who killed due to obedience to authority. Goldhagen believed they were specifically "ordinary Germans" who killed because historic anti-Semitism built the desire to eliminate Jews. Both may have been partially correct in their assumptions. As other studies have shown, obedience to authority lends itself to allowing genocide, which supported Browning. It was, however, missing the target of the hate. Goldhagen's supposition was supported by the strong underlying antisemitism, but antisemitism was not exclusive to Germany. Both authors agreed the participants of the killings had the choice to refuse, but many took part with sadistic enthusiasm.

While there were soldiers/guards who asked for transfers or later committed suicide, many continued helping with the Final Solution. One explanation was the public shared a "Nazi Mind" which might rationalize why so many willingly participated. Until the 1960s, British and American psychologists tried to define the psychological deficiency, however, "Nazi Mind" was undefinable. Adolf Eichmann's psychological evaluation, while he awaited trial and eventual execution, put an end to the hunt for a psychological deficiency. Psychologists who studied Eichmann found individuals who committed those atrocities weren't required to be "sadistic monsters."

Hannah Arendt, a German philosopher who attended the trial, observed, *"The trouble with Eichmann was precisely that so many were like him...that they were, and still are, terribly and terrifyingly normal."*

Many scholars attempted to answer whether the perpetrators fundamentally differed from the general population. As much as the scholars tried to find a distinction, they reached dead ends in demonizing the perpetrators. Whether the offenders be high-ranking officers who set the policies or the rank-and-file who carried out their orders, no definitive impairments, or the elusive "Nazi Mind" was found. Only a small number of the rank-and-file showed extraordinary psychopathology. Some displayed unusual thought patterns in terms of being rigid and pessimistic, but not to a disturbed level. Researchers learned the perpetrators were extraordinary in what they'd done, but not in who they were. Research showed no indication of mental impairment and no identifiers that the offenders were sadists at home nor in social settings. The perpetrators came from all walks of life, all personality types, and all age groups. Many of them were not politically active nor associated with social groups focused on institutionalizing destructive processes. They truly were a cross-section of average human beings.

The descent into becoming a mass murderer in most cases was done in increments and through the nature of the collective, which tended to bring out the worst in people.

Gustave LeBon observed, *"The mere fact that he forms part of an organized crowd, a man descends several rungs in the ladder of civilization. Isolated, he may be a cultivated individual; in a crowd, he is a barbarian—that is a creature acting on instinct."*

Freud noted when individuals were grouped, they lost their opinions and intellectual faculties and lost control of their feelings and instincts. An individual's actions within the group would've surprised the person and those who knew them. As an individual joins a group, moral constraints weaken, and diffusion of responsibility eases the immoral act.

Often, offender groups went through gradual desensitization which devolved into killing. The groups took part in an escalating of brutality that eventually led to carnage. Through peer pressure, conformity, camaraderie, diffusion of responsibility, and a culturally rewarding cruelty, the group formed strong bonds. The process of indoctrination to mayhem within the formed group created a feeling within each member of not wanting to disappoint the group. The attacks took on a feeling of choreography and that no one wished to disrupt. One assailant stated at the first killing, he felt nauseated but didn't step out of line because he didn't want to disrupt the process. Some described the slaying as "theatre" or "ceremony". This feeling of a theatre or ceremony increased as the victims were seen as mostly following the script by complying with the process. The mass murder of the Jewish population became part of the group's daily routine. Many thought their actions weren't wrong or criminal, it was their duty.

An ethnic German who helped rescue many Jewish people had a chance to interact with German guards at concentration camps. In an interview, he relayed a conversation he had with a guard.

"I interviewed many SS guards. I was always intrigued by the question, 'How could seemingly normal people become killers?' Once, I got an interesting answer. In a camp in upper Silesia, I asked one of our guards, pointing at the big gun in his holster, 'Did you ever use that to kill?' He replied, 'Once I had to shoot six Jews. I did not like that at all, but when you get such an order, you have to be hard.' Then he

added, 'You know they were not human anymore.' That was the key— dehumanization. You first call your victim names and take away his dignity. You restrict his nourishment, and he loses his physical beauty and sometimes some of his moral values. You take away soap and water, then say the Jew stinks. Then you take their human dignity further away by putting them in situations where they even will do such things which are criminal. Then you take food away. Then they lose their beauty and health and so on, they are not human anymore. When he's reduced to a skin-colored skeleton, you have taken away his humanity. It is much easier to kill non-humans than humans."

Many executors, like my grandfather, returned to normal life at the end of the war as if nothing had happened. A perpetrator seldom sees themselves as a criminal. They don't see it as a career choice since they believe their actions are only temporarily needed. They see their actions as merely doing their part at the time, due to little-or-no control over their circumstances. The Holocaust participants saw their actions as "celebrating what is right", not as strict obedience to authority. In the end, many resorted to denial, rationalization, and righteous anger toward the Jews for creating the mess.

While many went back to living normal lives, they were forced to hide their actions and their views on the Jewish extermination. The Germans would not have parades celebrating their generals. Governments passed laws that outlawed symbols of the Nazi regime. Society made the German offenders pariahs and their actions and ideals unacceptable.

While there were some who tried holding to Nazi ideology, the open organized movement, witnessed in some former Confederate states, did not occur. Antisemitism continued in Germany after the Holocaust atrocities, but not the sustained violent and terroristic acts witnessed in WWII. Violence against the Jewish population has been more sporadic without societal support. In former Confederate states, lynching, Jim Crow laws, and violent segregation of southern Blacks continued decades after the Civil War ended. Many laws needed to end racial violence were not passed until eighty years later. Open support for subjugation methods and violence witnessed at the end of the Civil War was not seen in Germany after WWII. In fact, the desire to deny atrocities the Nazis and German people inflicted on the Jews may have helped Germany and other countries limit continued violence and discrimination.

Offenders lived normal lives. Their children, who were too young to remember the war or were born after the war, undoubtedly were not regaled with stories of the parents' murderous exploits. Families of war criminals who were arrested decades after World War II were surprised by the accusations. They often vehemently denied their loved one was the monster they were accused of being. The mass murderers were able to blend into society and put their war-time actions behind them. The fact that the perpetrators went on to live productive, seemingly ordinary lives made it harder to see the monsters hidden inside.

A danger in trying to understand why people act a certain way is one can appear to be looking for excuses for their actions. A social psychological study found even minimal exposure to explanations might cause a shift in judgment toward more lenient opinions on the killers.

Social psychologist Roy Baumeister explained, *"It is a mistake to let moral condemnation interfere with trying to understand—but it would be a bigger mistake to let that understanding, once it had been attained, interfere with moral condemnation."*

The killers were not victims of fate and had options other than participating in murder. Killing innocent people is inexcusable. The ease in which perpetrators transformed from everyday people to mass murderers, and back to normal was concerning and unsettling. When underlying hate is held in check, it takes little for that hate to grow to dangerous levels and spread.

While I understood more of the dynamics which contributed to the Holocaust and how perpetrators lived guilt-free afterward, the knowledge did little to help me understand my grandfather. I was left with disappointment my grandfather was not one who asked for a job reassignment or who lived under Nazi occupation the best they could. I felt pain for what he put them through and sorrow for the lives he took. I don't know if the psychological studies found a "Nazi mind" to explain his behavior would've made me feel better. It would be easy to say he was a product of the time, but there were numerous examples of heroes living at the same time who risked their lives to help the Jewish population.

As I read about my grandfather's past and researched mass murderers attempting to understand my grandfather, I realized the search put me on an emotional and psychological rollercoaster. Not all my pursuit was centered around coming to grips with my grandfather's past. It made me wonder if, after so many decades, there would be lingering impacts on future generations. I knew it impacted survivors, but what about their descendants and the perpetrators' descendants? Could an occurrence that happened prior to one's birth or when they were too young to understand have an impact on their mental health and worldview beyond those whose families were not directly impacted by genocide?

Chapter 8 ~ The Lingering Effects of Hate

After all, when a stone is dropped into a pond, the water continues quivering even after the stone has sunk to the bottom.
—Arthur Golden

When genocides are brought to an end and perpetrators are brought to justice, one often senses a feeling of accomplishment. There is a general feeling of wellbeing when tormented victims are saved and extreme hatred has been vanquished. Even though groups may display hate toward another, like Neo-Nazis, their power to inflict pain on others without repercussions has been greatly reduced. Society understands those who are traumatized by offenders may have long-term mental and physical health problems due to direct or indirect stress they experienced.

Not until a decade after World War II was the impact of trauma on survivors' mental health, particularly those of the Holocaust, studied. That understanding helped create methods of helping future victims of genocide. The studies led to the additional study of the survivors' descendants in what is now known as transgenerational or historical trauma. Research psychologists have found trauma is not only being seen in those who suffered extreme hate, in various forms, trauma's effects are passed to their descendants. Transgenerational/intergenerational trauma is not only being seen in the victims' descendants, but in the perpetrators' descendants, as well. Transgenerational trauma's effect on future generations is an important reason to stop the spread of hate.

The DSM-5 categorizes a traumatized person as one who may have been a direct victim of the act of aggression, witnessed or learned about the act against someone close to them, or repeatedly exposed to the details of the aggression. When it comes to large-scale aggression against a group of people, that can cause numerous people to become traumatized. Due to the large number of people impacted over several years, the Holocaust survivors became the focus of research on the impact of systemic aggression. After World War II, research on psychological impacts of concentration camp survivors were performed. One of the first syndromes identified by researchers was post-concentration camp asthenia. Those suffering from post-concentration camp asthenia displayed symptoms of somatic complaints, such as headaches and chest pains, neuropsychological disturbances, such as anxiety, depression, and suicidal ideations, cognitive impairments, such as memory and concentration problems, and disruption of social and interpersonal functioning in terms of withdrawal and alienation. Most survivors who suffered from the syndrome developed distrust towards others, increased arousal and hypervigilance, and lower general life dynamics. Some displayed opposite symptoms, however, including trust to the point of naivety.

As studies of the Holocaust survivors continued, mental health impacts from trauma became better defined. For example, the psychological term "survivor syndrome" was introduced in the 1960s. Some symptoms of survivor syndrome are the same as post-concentration camp asthenia. Both include anxiety, depression, and memory disturbances, but survivor syndrome includes pervasive survivor guilt and alterations of personal identity. Research of Holocaust victims essentially found many of the victims dealt with mental health issues because of the torment they endured. Today, Holocaust survivors would be diagnosed with the more commonly known post-traumatic stress disorder (PTSD). The symptoms of PTSD include those defined in the post-concentration camp asthenia and survivor syndrome and is used to diagnose any person who has endured trauma that has lasting psychological effects.

While many trauma survivors display varying degrees of mental health issues, some didn't develop any. For the Holocaust survivors who did, their experiences with aggression didn't cease with the perpetrators' conviction. Events in everyday life that may not have elicited a response from most people, might have triggered the survivor. An event may bring up feelings that seem unjustified to non-survivors. For example, survivors may have negative reactions to laws or law enforcement personnel since many of the aggressions against them were supported by laws and inflicted by those acting under the law.

For child survivors, those who were younger than sixteen when World War II ended, a slightly different set of mental health symptoms were addressed. While children are often seen as resilient after traumatic events, the level and duration of trauma the children experienced during their formative years would leave a mark on their mental health. The trauma impacted how they lived after the war ended.

Many Jewish children who survived the Holocaust did so because, as their parents were rounded up and removed, neighbors took the children into their homes. The Jewish children who didn't find refuge with another family were often immediately sent to the gas chambers. They couldn't perform the required work and were considered "useless eaters" by the Nazis. That meant many Jewish children who survived were raised by non-Jewish families. Their true identities were hidden, their names changed. For the children who survived the concentration camps, being dehumanized to a mere number robbed them of their identities. After the war, the children suffered from identity problems. Child survivors, especially those who survived the camps, learned to endure by taking on certain behaviors, which they exhibited throughout the rest of their lives, such as passivity, helplessness, a belief in an external control, and identifying themselves as the "victim".

While the children who survived the Holocaust experienced survivor guilt or "survivor syndrome", they also experienced feelings of rejection, loneliness, and worthlessness. As the children grew into adults, those feelings caused them to strongly react to threats of separation, whether real or imagined. Since they were snatched from their parents, either when left with another family or at the camps, their reactions were understandable. Many children never saw their parents again. The child survivors also showed signs of chronic grief reactions, withdrawal from social situations, and difficulty trusting others. The children either suffered from amnesia and emotional numbing about their experiences, or they formed a trauma fixation. Neither response lent itself to healing from trauma, which they would carry into adulthood.

Whether an adult or child survivor, after the war many attempted to live normal lives by starting families, either with a fellow survivor or a new family. Trauma survivors experience changed their behavior toward the outside world. As the survivors procreated, their behaviors and views impacted how they taught their children to interact in the world.

The impact on the descendants of survivors of major traumatic events can increase when trauma is carried by a cultural group. This means trauma is not just passed on through the parents' behaviors, but also through their culture through stories, myths, new cultural norms, and institutions.

Trauma's ripple effect has been referred to as intergenerational trauma, historical trauma, and secondary/vicarious traumatization. It comes from severe trauma such as war, dislocation, enslavement, and genocide cultural groups have been subjected to. Then consequences of the trauma get passed down through future generations. The study of intergenerational trauma started with Holocaust survivors and their children, but, as time went on, children of other genocides, Vietnam Veterans, and domestic violence were included.

The phenomenon of transgenerational trauma was recognized in the 1990s as a mental health issue. Transgenerational trauma has been observed in not only the survivors' descendants but also in professionals who've worked with survivors and in the U.S. Holocaust Memorial Museum employees. The impacted museum employees demonstrate direct contact with survivors is not necessary to experience traumatic event's mental health impact, but can occur working with documentation, photographs, and objects associated with the event.

Even when survivors remain quiet about their experienced trauma, the impacts can be passed on to their descendants. While survivors may try to overcome their pasts by burying experiences and feelings, their actions and interactions with others will betray the damage done. Schwab stated:

"It is the children or descendants ... who will be haunted by what is buried in this tomb, even if they do not know of its existence or contents and even if the history that produced the ghost is shrouded in silence. Often the tomb is a familial one, organized around family secrets shared by parents and perhaps grandparents but fearfully guarded from the children. It is through the unconscious transmission of disavowed familial dynamics that one generation affects another generation's unconscious. This unconscious transmission is ... the dynamics of transgenerational haunting."

A study on Holocaust survivors' descendants found that even in persons who've not experienced more personal trauma than that of a comparison group, they suffered at a higher rate from PTSD symptoms and other mental health disorders. That meant the Holocaust survivors' children who've had a "normal" childhood without a higher level of direct trauma than their peers showed more trauma symptoms as if they had. The level of the descendants' symptoms was found to directly correlate with the severity of the parent's PTSD symptoms. The more severe the symptoms in the parent, the more trauma symptoms were seen in the descendants. More recent studies into the third generation (grandchildren) of survivors found there were psychological differences when compared to their peers.

While much of the intergenerational trauma research had been centered around Holocaust survivors' families, mass traumatic events' lingering impacts were found elsewhere. Blacks within the United States were one of the groups shown to have intergenerational trauma. Trauma perpetuated to the current generation came from over a century of slavery followed by decades of segregation and Jim Crow laws. Not surprising, those who suddenly found themselves freed didn't receive any support. If a similar situation happened today, organized groups would avail themselves to help with the freed citizens' psychological and physical needs as they transitioned. Understanding the needs of traumatized people and how PTSD impacts them is greater today than even fifty years ago. Juxtaposed to over a century ago when newly freed people were targeted with hate and violence, including rape, castrations, and lynching.

Due to the uniqueness of continued behavioral impacts from slavery trauma, the term post-traumatic slave syndrome has been created. The term explains the transmission of trauma leads to behaviors associated with increased anger, lower self-esteem, passivity, mistrust, and feelings of inferiority found in Blacks in America. The study suggests enslaved people who witnessed abuse by owners of slaves who demonstrated aggressiveness became traumatized. Transgenerational trauma passed through future generations, even though they had never witnessed slavery or abuse. The enslaved people taught their offspring to forge nonthreatening identities, contrary to a natural response to oppression, so that they could better survive. The teachings created a cultural requirement to instruct children to be subdued, to obey the system, and to mistrust anyone outside their group.

While the Emancipation Proclamation was signed into law almost 160 years ago, continued racism and violence against Blacks perpetuate post-traumatic slave syndrome.

Researchers of the syndrome noted that, *"[T]he persistent presence of racism, despite the significant legal, social, and political progress made during the last half of the twentieth century, has created a physiological risk for black people that is virtually unknown to white America."*

Black children, particularly males, are taught by their predecessors to take a passive, overly respectful stance when interacting with law enforcement and other authority figures. While survival behaviors developed over a century ago by their ancestors may have been passed on, the behaviors' emotional impacts might be less if not for continued Black-focused racism and violence. Racism, violence, and intergenerational poverty feeds Blacks' traumatic stress, which then regenerates the idea black children need to be taught their ancestors' survival behaviors.

Ancestors need not endure centuries of trauma to cause intergenerational trauma. Atrocities lasting a year or two can have intergenerational impacts. Throughout history, descendants of genocide survivors have been impacted in varying degrees from genocide-induced trauma. The determining factor of that degree seemed to depend more on the victim group's specific abuse, not the duration of the abuse. The symptoms were somewhat the same, but some differ in the genocidal events and lingering discrimination.

Studies show that over a century later, the slaughter of Armenians by Turks (from 1915 to 1917) impacts subsequent generations. Armenian genocide survivor's descendants report feelings of sadness, psychic pain carrying emotional memories, and helplessness. Effects of the atrocities committed against Armenians continue to be passed through future generations. The drive Armenians have to resuscitate their culture's history may be because the Turkish government continues to deny the Armenian population's genocide. Stories of Turkish atrocities have become part of Armenian culture. The inclusion of the horrific stories has reportedly given descendants nightmares about their ancestors' massacres. Armenian's continued oppression might add to their trauma-based nightmares. The Turkish government's deeds during the genocide and continued oppression of Armenian people who received little-to-no assistance, has led Armenians to become a closed group who has a strong mistrust of the Turkish population as well as other cultures. The Armenian population feels weak and vulnerable which causes them to view outside cultures as dangerous. Lack of reconciliation and distrust of other cultures might cause a group to violently react against real or perceived threats. An acknowledgement by the Turkish government could go a long way toward healing wounds, however, admitting transgressions, even after a century, can be difficult.

In addition to mistrusting outsiders, genocide changes the people's behavior in how they approach their daily lives. From 1932-1933, Russians invaded Ukraine. Russians committed genocide by cutting off the Ukrainians' access to food. The atrocity became known as the Holodomor Genocide. While descendants of Holodomor survivors saw the behaviors as irrational, those behaviors have become embedded in their culture. The main behavior unsurprisingly revolves around food. Ukrainians are known for stockpiling food, having a reverence for food, and overeating. They also have difficulties discarding unwanted items as the items might be later used for bartering. They harbor an indifference toward others as survival during Holodomor depended on taking care of oneself and one's family.

While many people stockpile food for emergencies such as natural disasters, the levels Ukrainians take their stockpiling is beyond what may be needed for a short period. One descendant described her stockpiling as:

"We once purchased a lot of salt. We had not managed to consume this salt over a period of years living in our original apartment. We transported this salt to our new apartment. Plain rock salt. Similarly, I remember a surplus of sugar and flour in sacks in her [great-grandmother] attic. This surplus was prepared and stored at regular intervals of frequency. This is yet another example of the consequences. This is what my grandmother did. This is what my mother did."

Stockpiling food is part of their culture. Not much thought is given to why they feel the need to store large quantities of staples. They state they need to ensure starvation will never occur again. A third-generation descendant of a Holodomor survivor described their reverence for food as follows:

"The Holodomor made this valuing of bread even more extreme. A piece of bread can save a person from hunger if you eat just a little bit. Then, when I traveled outside of Ukraine, I realized that this is only prevalent in Ukraine. This safeguarding and sacredness of bread.

Beyond our borders, people can throw bread away. For me, this was a genuine shock. Then, later I understood that people who have not experienced such a thing or whose ancestors did not survive such an experience, have a completely different frame of reference."

Other survivors noted they didn't notice Holodomor's impact on their behaviors and views until they traveled outside Ukraine. Some observed when traveling in other countries, their survival-mode mentality faded as those around them were not behaving in such a way.

When it comes to understanding mental health impacts on descendants of genocide survivors, the impacts may not be diagnosed until the descendants seek professional treatment.

Knowing what survivors endured makes the transmission of trauma to their descendants obvious. It is difficult to imagine that surviving torture and genocide would not impact the survivor's children and future generations. Another type of victim of major hate events are the participant's descendants, however, they often are overlooked. Sympathy toward perpetrators' children is often absent, as focus is on victims and their families.

In a volume of papers presented at the Congress on "Children - In War and Persecution" in 1993, editors of the volume added the following preamble to the paper Children of Victims - Children of Perpetrators: *"Children of victims as well as of perpetrators are highly burdened by their parents' heritage. Whereas society tends to support and help children of victims, children of perpetrators experience different reactions."*

The impact on perpetrators' descendants is a little more complicated as it includes their parents' actions and society's disgust of the perpetrators.

Overlooking any mental impact, the children of perpetrators exclusion may be derived from the idea the children might follow in their parents' footsteps. While Nazi children's indoctrination continued until war's end caused some, like the daughters of Himmler and Goering, to identify with their parents' ideology, others took measures to distance themselves. Hermann Goering's great-niece and great-nephew opted to be sterilized so the Goering name would die with them. Whether the children were alive and cognizant of Nazi propaganda or too young or born after the Holocaust, they suffered from their ancestors' crimes. The descendants have, however, often suffered in silence due to the stigma of those crimes, whether committed by an uncle, grandfather, father, or brother.

Many children growing up during the Holocaust were shielded from atrocities of adults. Those who lived at or near concentration camps were not exposed to crimes occurring within the camps, even though some had prisoners working in their homes. Assaults that the men took part in went unspoken within their families. While family members were unaware of the camp prisoners' maltreatment or the actions of family men, boys were often placed in Hitler Youth programs and girls into The League of German Girls to be taught to be good Nazis. That created an aura the men in their families were good men and good Nazis.

Ranking Nazi children's lives reflected their relative's status, who were often highly respected by their peers. Their personal home lives were seen as normal anywhere in the world. Some lived in households with loving fathers, others with authoritative, distant fathers. Either way, they enjoyed privileges that came with being the child of a respected Nazi.

Children who were old enough to enjoy increased status endured a confusing time at the Third Reich's fall. A child's loss of continuity was difficult, especially when their father was arrested for his crimes.

An SS officer's daughter summed up the impact on children when she said, *"I was nobody now."*

In addition to losing their identity in society, some children also lost their homes and means to live. That would cause trauma to any child regardless of the situation. Those children had the added trauma of learning what their fathers were doing.

One child of a convicted war criminal struggled to reconcile the father who loved her with the man convicted of war crimes. She stated:

"This is so hard to live with. He is the father I have loved so much, who made me feel so loved, and he is now the father whom I hate for what he has done. How can I have any respect for him? Yet I still love him. That is why my head is splitting. I can't keep these two fathers together. And I don't know where this puts me."

Children of perpetrators have difficulty perceiving the loving father in their world after learning of the monstrous actions in another. They try to protect the caring father of their childhood while also denying crimes their parent committed. Children also question their self-image since their father had two seemingly different personas. For children who did not have a loving father, accepting their parent's conviction and lack of remorse at breaking contact with their father was easier. Those who had a loving relationship with their father were unable to maintain affection unless they were able to create a separation between the parent and the monster. Children able to create a separation found some semblance of healing.

What makes it more difficult for children and those who follow to avoid trauma is the silence about the perpetrators' crimes and the rewriting of family history that follows. The German society created an "endorsed amnesia" through the censoring of discussions on the Holocaust following the war. There was no public taking of responsibility for the crimes nor any public admission of regret or guilt. Anything related to the Holocaust was suppressed.

The child of a Holocaust perpetrator noticed the reaction to debating the event was one of defensiveness. The person was told to "just move on with your life." She observed the German population had not moved on. They continued to be in a state of denial and disengaged from life.

With a desire to distance themselves from the Holocaust crimes, families created false histories, including helping the Jews survive instead of participating in their destruction. That meant an implausibly high number of non-Jewish German families worked against the Nazis. Those who didn't claim to help the Jews created a history of innocent onlookers and placed blame on other Germans. Family histories falsely identified their ancestors who lived in those areas during the war knew nothing of the genocide, so none should feel shame or guilt.

Many non-Jewish German families had a rule barring children from asking what family members did during the war. My grandparents followed that rule, as my mother was discouraged from asking questions and soon stopped trying. Creating a taboo around the discussion of the war created an ominous cloud over the role my family may have played in the Holocaust. Sharing stories is a way humans form relationships. By creating a large void in story sharing, descendants develop a fear of intimacy and have life-long relationship issues. The descendants learn to separate information about themselves, creating a wall which hinders their relationship-building abilities.

Relatives admitted at times to having family members who were Nazis. The role of the Nazi, however, was often downplayed. The person was often depicted as a "good" Nazi who helped Germany and took no part in the Holocaust. In one instance, a grandfather was seen as a resistance fighter who signed Jews' deportation orders to labor camps to avoid being murdered. One Nazi's grandchildren were told he was a "decent" Nazi, a mere victim of the system, not the victimizer. The truth was his involvement contributed to the deaths of sixty-five thousand Slovak Jews. Nazi and non-Jewish families often repeated that common narrative although records on the family member's role could easily be found and harder to deny when family members were convicted of their crimes.

In addition to the benign narrative, the perpetrators were often excused as a "victim of the time", while the impact on survivors was ignored. Family histories were often filled with hardship stories due to the war, such as male family members killed in action, city bombings, and, in western Germany, the Russian atrocities committed on the German population. The roles non-Jewish German families played in deporting and killing Jews was not discussed as many of them portrayed themselves as the victims of war.

As information came out, perpetrators' family members were shocked and shamed and left with emotional consequences stemming from confusion about their family's history. When the family's history was fully revealed, it caused rifts within families. The delayed learning of the truth was equated to "waking up into a nightmare". Their idyllic family was suddenly invaded by monsters.

Family members who don't fully know the crimes of their ancestor might create a narrative where their ancestor did not actively participate in the atrocities to maintain a positive image of their beloved predecessor. That can be a way for those with loving parents or grandparents to avoid dealing with the conflicting vastly different visions of the same person. It can also help deal with the guilt of loving someone whose actions were seen as evil. One granddaughter who, much like me, after accidentally learning about her grandfather's history tried to convince herself her dear "gramps" was not a war criminal. She told herself that her SS grandfather worked in a hospital caring for soldiers and not associated with the murders of Jews. Many of the Holocaust descendants fear that if their ancestor was involved in evil, they themselves may somehow be tainted or evil. By trying to create a difference, they alleviate fears about themselves and uncomplicate the loyalty they feel toward their ancestor.

Those whose family history is murky, not knowing their ancestors' roles during the Holocaust may cause feelings of shame and guilt. Many non-Jewish German people directly or indirectly participated in the Holocaust, at various levels. That knowledge causes descendants to consider their ancestors probably had a hand in genocide, the extent of which is unknown. That can cause more shame and guilt as they fantasize what dark family secrets there may be.

The perpetrators' crimes leave many of their descendants dealing with a tarnished history. In addition to shame and guilt, hatred of the perpetrator and what they represented comes full force. The hatred, however, is complicated by a caring relationship between the perpetrator and the relative.

One person put it as:

"...for to remain fixed in hatred and fear of one's parents, one's first objects of love, is to risk emotional stultification, or even death, but to give in to impulses of attachment and affection, when they are directed towards parents who have committed horrific crimes, and who have done so not out of passion but from conviction and belief— to accept this is surely to give up a part of one's own moral being."

The mixed feelings in the descendants of the perpetrators leads them to prove they are unlike their ancestors. Some work at repressing any seemly aggressive or authoritative thought or behavior essentially becoming pacifists. Others work to identify with the victims by forming relationships with those in the victimized group. That can lead to marrying a Jewish person or converting to Judaism to prove they are nothing like the perpetrator.

Added into the mix of emotions that come with being a perpetrator's descendant, is the knowledge evil is not as distant as some wish. Descendants of perpetrators know there's a kernel of evil in all of us. The knowledge impacts their ability to trust others.

As Niklas Frank, son of Hans Frank, the governor of Poland and known as the "Butcher of Poland," warned an audience of Germans:

81

"I don't trust any of you. Who knows? If the economy turns bad again, you might get those ideas again, to follow a strong leader, restrict ethnic minorities, maybe even imprison them. You don't have to call it 'concentration camps.' Here and there you have a little murder, a little killing. It might help purify the bloodline. Besides, it will create more jobs for real Germans."

His warning can be applied to any community of perpetrators' descendants, especially those who originally knew the perpetrators as loving, caring family members. The knowledge of an ancestor's past instills in them the belief that even if someone appears to be a good, loving person, evil hidden within may reveal itself under the right circumstances. With that wisdom comes obstacles to the ability of fully trusting others, even within their family.

While more understanding of trauma on an individual's mental health and the therapy availabilities to help survivors of trauma exist, impacts on their descendants can be overlooked. That's especially true for perpetrators' descendants as focus remains on victims and their descendants. While the perpetrators' descendants tend to remain silent, the damage is real and should be addressed.

While researching intergenerational trauma on the descendants of the perpetrators of genocide, particularly the Holocaust, I began to understand my mother's behavior and some of my own. Combined with the six years my mother spent in an internment camp, the secrets my grandparents kept impacted her mental health. I found reassurance reading about other descendants who grappled with their ancestors' crimes. Reading other descendants' stories of emotional battles that mirrored feelings I struggled with and am still struggling with was somewhat comforting. Knowledge that trauma's impact ripples through generations highlights that more needs to be done to stop hate before it grows and spreads to sadistic levels. Society not only needs to step up after the results of extreme hate to heal wounds but needs to step up against its growth. That's not an easy task, but with today's technology and the ability to connect to large numbers of people in different geographical locations, becoming an assertive world society against hate is more important than ever.

Chapter 9 ~ Social Media - The Superspreader of Hate

Hate crimes are the scariest thing in the world because these people really believe what they're doing is right. —Cher

The internet and social media represent a double-edged sword. The internet increased our world's communication by instantaneously sending electronic messages. Social media has allowed people to stay connected across distances. While for most people, social media and the internet is a positive aspect of our current lives, some use these tools to spread hate and misinformation that can lead to animosity. With easy access to the internet, free social media applications, and limited controls, the online environment can foster a breeding ground and easy recruiting environment for groups of all kinds, including hate groups.

When my grandfather hid his past, his options for spreading hate were limited to person-to-person contact. Talking to the wrong person or caught handing out hate material could mean being found and arrested. In today's world, we have the means to anonymously make statements seen worldwide. That makes it difficult to stem the spread of hate within societies, and, in fact, has become a superspreader of hate.

Even prior to the internet, mainstream media caused hate-based violence. For example, an article in the Tulsa Tribune titled, "Nab Negro for Attacking Girl in Elevator" was authored by the Tulsa Tribune staff, and an editorial entitled, "To Lynch a Negro Tonight" were published in 1921. The article and editorial, which called for the slaying of a black man arrested for allegedly assaulting a white woman elevator operator, led to the Tulsa Race Massacre. A hate-baited mob destroyed forty blocks of Tulsa known as Black Wall Street and killed over three hundred people.

Germans spread their ideology about Jewish people being subhuman and the root of the Germany's problems by radio. In Rwanda, the genocide of millions of Tutsis and moderate Hutus were fueled by hateful misinformation spread by radio.

The internet has taken the communication across distances to millions of people to a new level. Its design makes it difficult to monitor.

The internet was created by Tim Berners-Lee in the early 1990s as a communication system difficult to control or destroy from a central point. The internet was seen as a way to quickly facilitate communication across vast distances and bring cultures together. Due to the internet's design, the problem arose when it was discovered there was no way to limit who communicates and what is communicated. While Berners-Lee's dream was for a place that provided users freedom to create and communicate, he admitted his dream became a nightmare when used to exacerbate hate speech.

The introduction of hate into the online world started in 1995 when the white-supremacist group, Stormfront, created a website to publish their ideologies. Stormfront's website quickly grew, becoming an example to other groups as to the internet's potential. Soon, other hate-filled websites were created, which allowed groups to advertise their ideologies to larger audiences without geographical constraints, granting easier recruitment of new members.

A former Ku Klux Klan Grand Wizard stated, *"[The internet has] been a tremendous boon for us. That's why I dedicate most of my time to this. I feel like I've accomplished more on the web than in my twenty-five years of political activism. Whereas before, we could reach only people with pamphlets or holding rallies with no more than a few hundred people, now we can reach potentially millions."*

While the internet opened the ability to create websites viewed by millions, social media took the ability to share information further. Instead of having a website only viewed by those who sought specific information, social media gave the ability to widely spread ideas. Additionally, social media has replaced newspapers and news programs as to where people get information about local and world events. During a crisis, accurate information is often in short supply. Information found on social media platforms, whether accurate or not, addresses the need for immediate edification. In social media, data is spread through sharing one's own and other's posts. As users scroll through their feeds, they see information shared by others. While many times, this is enjoyable, light-hearted information, the possibility of some level of a hate post appearing on a person's newsfeed is present.

Exposure to cyberhate has increased and has been the subject of several studies. One study found twenty-four percent of Americans report frequent exposure to cyberhate and forty-one percent report occasionally being exposed. A study done in five European countries indicated the range of exposure went from sixty-four-point-five percent in France to seventy-five percent in Finland. The most disturbing statistic was the rise of cyberhate exposure among American youth and young adults between 2013 to 2016. The results concluded an increase in exposure from fifty-three to seventy percent. Exposure improves a hate group's ability to recruit new members as it is seen as one of the first steps towards radicalization.

When newspaper publishing increased, Danish philosopher, Soren Kierkegaard-Qualms, expressed his view the press separated knowledge from experience by making knowledge available to those who may not have the experience in the topic they read about. The internet has exacerbated that by availing people with information on every topic, whether reputable or not, but also anonymously allows people of limited knowledge and experience to post information. The feeling of anonymity has been shown to embolden people to publicly publish online what they may not say in person, which allows for all extremists' views, good or bad, to be readily shared.

An insidious aspect of social media is its ability to permit people to remain anonymous. Few controls exist barring a person from creating accounts with fake names or, on some platforms, nonsensical screen names. The anonymous aspect of social media led to users referred to as trolls. Social media allows trolls to anonymously harass people in public forums. Trolls make deviant comments they would not make in public as they would most likely be ostracized by society. Using anonymity, trolls feel they can safely say racially biased and bigoted remarks meant to upset or terrorize and find others with similar mindsets.

While at first trolls may have been individuals looking to harass people and spread hate, some countries and organizations have created "troll farms" that allow them to dictate information seen by social media users. Troll farms can be an army of users who spread misinformation on a variety of topics, such as elections and the pandemic. Additionally, internet programs, called bots, are created to rapidly create posts. Troll farms utilize bots to harass people and spread misinformation that manipulates peoples' opinions and views. The farms often exploit a person's fears or uncertainties as fertile grounds upon which to grow misinformation. People who fear more readily believe information that feeds their fears. Additionally, when information is repetitious, such as the information dispersed by bot farms, the information's credibility increases in people's minds. Once reports start to sound real, it's difficult for people to later accept facts.

Countries where the government controls internet content, bot farms help amass regime support, as well as quash any opposition. That spread of misinformation has been seen in Russia in terms of the Russian's views on the Ukrainian government. The Russian government spread information that Ukraine was being overrun by Nazis, and the Ukrainian president was a Nazi. As Zelenskyy is Jewish, him being a Nazi is absurd and overlooked by many Russians. When the invasion of Ukraine began, Ukrainians who spoke to their Russian relatives could not convince them that what they were being told were lies. The only information to which the Russians had access (unless they were tech savvy and set up connections outside Russia), continued to feed misinformation on potential harm Ukrainians could cause to Russia if not for the invasion.

Other countries have used the internet and social media to spread propaganda and indoctrinate people with false information.

Misinformation being presented to people on social media creates a false narrative of world events and what is socially acceptable which may cause some to adjust their behaviors. People's behavior in society is in-part based on accepted social norms. Within the social media realm, what is considered acceptable can become skewed due to social media algorithms used to limit a person's access and what they see on their newsfeed. Due to our internet searches, groups we join, and other postings, what we see on our newsfeed had been algorithmically adjusted to fall in line with our preferences. The adjustments cause a person's newsfeed to show items supporting their views and create a feeling of community corroboration that is at times falsely augmented.

Social media companies collect data on their customers' visited internet sites, posted contents, liked social media pages, and joined groups to create data sets that allow for user information micro-targeting. The targeting consists of information based on collected data the platform feels the user most wants to see. The process adds to information inundation that lends support to a person's ideology and the feeling of not being an outlier in their beliefs as they see more posts that support their views. Micro-targeting can be used by organizations who pay to get their posts seen by people they believe want to see them. While this can be helpful for people to find services, it's a tool that can be used by groups to recruit more members, including hate groups. Again, showing the double-edged sword of social media.

In 2018, Facebook announced they adjusted their algorithms to place posts with the more likes, comments, and shares at the top of customer's feeds. A problem with that is negative posts and posts that play with one's emotions, like anger or fear, tend to get more user interaction causing the posts to be pushed higher on the user's news feeds. That means posts that feed hate, whether the post is openly hateful or not, will be seen more by a user who interacted to similar posts. Those with unacceptable ideologies may feel their personal views have more support than they have in reality, as their newsfeed becomes inundated with posts supporting their views. Some users don't understand the immense number of members in the social media community. When they see a post with a tens of thousands of likes and a few thousand comments, they might be misled into feeling that the post's point of view has widespread support. What they do not realize is the post has only a minuscule percent support from the social media community.

If virtual hate communities' activities remained online, the damage they could cause would be minimal. While psychological harm can be damaging to targeted individuals, online hate may be turning into physically harmful actions due to deceptive community support indicated by adjusted algorithms.

A study on the link between online hate and public violence, when looking at attacks on refugees in Germany, has indicated there are causal effects. A fifty percent increase in attacks was noted with a one-standard deviation increase in anti-refugee content on social media. There was a drop in refugee attacks in Germany when Facebook availability was disrupted in a high-Facebook usage area. The drop in attacks was at a similar rate as the rise in attacks with the increase in Facebook usage.

With social media users receiving posts that mirror their personal world views and often visiting pages and sites which mimic their belief systems, social media and the internet can become what is called an "echo chamber" for all users. An echo chamber is where the user sees only information consistent with their ideologies and can further push them towards like-minded groups, including those that advocate hate. The impact of echo chambers is seen in real-life events.

One major example was the occurrence on January 6, 2021. In addition to the riot, or insurrection, planned on social media platforms, some participants may have been indoctrinated through information shared on social media and news outlets regarding the outcome of the election, and they were compelled to do the "right" thing. During the January 6th hearings, one of the participants testified that based on what he had read on social media, he believed he acted as a U.S. patriot. It wasn't until he got off social media that he saw how he was misled. He realized it wasn't likely the judges who turned down election-corruption lawsuits were in cahoots. He had to step out of his echo chamber to see he was misled.

Those in the justice system witness and understand the impact of hate rhetoric consumed online on the populace. The justice presiding over a case where a man drove his car into a group of Muslims in North London noted the impact of online material in radicalizing the perpetrator. The justice remarked that the large amount of online hate propaganda the perpetrator consumed fed his hate and mental vulnerabilities until he turned to violence. It was also noted how information was easily accessed that fed anger in mentally vulnerable people. Other cases of hate-fueled violence have been tied to online content either through having an audience with which to share their views and get validation or through reading hate-based content.

One would think stopping online hate would be as easy as denying social media access to those who spread hate. It is much more complicated, however, due to internet and social media platforms' designs. First, even when a user is banned for their posts, nothing prevents them from migrating to a different social media platform or creating a new account with a false name on the same platform.

One platform that has become a mecca for hate-oriented users is Gab. While small in terms of number of active users when compared to other social media platforms, Gab has found a strong following from those looking for a place to openly discuss their ideologies, including hate-based ones. Gab has billed itself as a "free speech" platform that champions individual liberties and the sharing of information. It has since become widely reported as a platform for all forms of bigotry and hate. The platform has claimed if the speech is "legal under U.S. law, it is allowed on our site". Since the Supreme Court rulings have rarely found speech they considered illegal, that left the door wide open for what some people can and do post on Gab.

The only posts that can cause a user to be banned are, "copyright infringements, illegal pornography, defamation, spam, and true threats." The enforcement of what constitutes a true threat can be difficult to determine until after an event, especially on a hate-speech filled platform that may refer to annihilating a group of people. In the case of the Pittsburgh synagogue shooting on October 27, 2018, the CEO of Gab did not consider the shooter's posts as threats that should have been reported prior to the shooting.

In addition to the numerous clearly bigoted and full of hate posts on Gab, the platform, as all platforms, shares news articles with its users. The articles tended to subtly support the stereotypical Gab user's ideologies, but supported certain views by leaning the articles in a way that made it appear there was a threat to freedom or a decay of morals. These articles do not outright use terms considered part of the "hate lexicon" but are written in a way that the hate message is made to those looking for support of their views.

Even on social media platforms that do not bill themselves as "free speech" havens, there is often little motivation to try to stop users from making hate-filled posts. Facebook, Twitter, and other social media platforms are free for people to use. That means the money to run these companies must come from somewhere. This money comes from outside investors who use a metric called "Daily Active Users" to determine the success or failure of social media platforms. In one quarter in 2018, Facebook had over 2.23 billion active users on its platform. The financial health of social media platforms is dependent on people using the platforms daily, which would discourage restricting or preventing individuals from using the platform.

In 2018, Facebook posts comparing Myanmar's Muslim minority to animals for raping citizens of the Buddhist majority appeared on over one thousand accounts. While some posts came from accounts belonging to known pop stars, a military hero, and a beauty queen, most were posted by the general population, some most likely using anonymous screen names. The posts contributed to thousands of Muslims, including children, being killed in Myanmar and almost 700,000 fleeing to neighboring Bangladesh. Facebook admitted it "can and should do more" after the backlash over allowing the initial posts.

In some countries, the ability for social media companies to operate within their borders is determined by those countries' rulers. In 2020, an Indian politician promoted the killing of Muslims by declaring they should be slaughtered. Other politicians added to his rhetoric by posting accusations that Muslims intentionally spread the coronavirus and married Hindu women as an attempt at "love Jihad". The posts were noted by Facebook employees as hate speech and the posters were warned that such posts could lead to violence due to the history of communal conflict within India. Rioting occurred after a lawmaker posted his supporters would "clear" those protesting a citizenship bill that excluded Muslims. The subsequent violence killed dozens of people who were mostly Muslim. A top lobbying Facebook executive in India warned Facebook staff if they applied hate speech rules to politicians and lawmakers, Facebook's ability to operate in India would be impaired. With India being an important market for Facebook, the threat of ceased operations in the country was financially detrimental.

Even within the United States, Facebook employees were hesitant to censor posts made by elected government officials. That has changed some since January 6th, but prior to then social media platforms were not inclined to apply the same rules of conduct to those in governmental positions as they did to the general public. During the January 6th hearings, a Twitter employee testified that the posts President Trump made prior to his election and once he was in office would not have been allowed had he had not been a celebrity. One example of leniency is when he posted "when the looting starts, the shooting starts" during the protests over George Floyd's death at the hand of police officers. While Twitter labeled the post with a warning that it violated the rules against glorifying violence, Facebook allowed the post to stand with no warnings or deletion because it came from a politician and was newsworthy. Prior to the George Floyd tweet, Twitter allowed other tweets that would have gotten other users suspended or banned. They also claimed the president's tweets were newsworthy because of his position. As we have seen throughout history, the open views of leaders can embolden their followers to act.

The "Trump-effect", caused by his divisive posts, created an increase in hate posts and hate crimes. While hate towards Muslims and immigrants was easy to feed and had been occurring before President Trump's election, his handling of the Coronavirus saw an increased hate towards Asians still being seen after he left office. The World Health Organization (WHO) recognized that what it names diseases has an impact on people's views. They issued guidelines that prohibit diseases from having names containing geographical locations, cultures, or populations. Following President Trump's use of the term "China virus" in a March 2020 tweet, the use of inflammatory names for the Coronavirus increased as people in power used the derogatory terms with impunity. As the terms were continually seen on social media, they became normalized and harder for most people to see as derogatory. There was also an increase in hate crimes and general hate against Asians in the United States. Even as the pandemic came under control and over a year after the change in presidency, Asians were targeted by hate. This indicates that once started, it's difficult to stop the tide of hate towards a group.

Usually, a person who is the target of a crime can take legal recourse against the person who committed the crime, and possibly others who assisted. In the United States, however, social media companies have no legal liability for user content posted on their sites. The Communications Defense Act Section 230 prevents victims of terrorist acts, which hate crimes could fall under, from seeking compensation from social media companies. The section makes the users liable for the content posted, not the provider of the service. In cases that have been filed, courts have interpreted the act as preventing every kind of civil lawsuit against companies for user content on their platforms. With no legal ramifications, there is no pressure for social media companies to curtail hateful comments beyond remaining in line with social morals.

Social media companies have employees whose jobs are monitoring posts and identifying those that contain hate speech. The use of humans is needed because those who spread hate are savvy enough to use terms an algorithm would not automatically identify as hate speech. A user avoids using targeted terms or explicitly call for the death of a person or someone in a group of people. Instead, they will use code words that others of similar ideology understand but slip past programs and human monitors. These posts contain ironic comments, rhetorical questions, or the use of emojis not necessarily seen as violating platform rules.

As one monitor stated, *"We often see comments in which experienced users refrain from using racist language, but nevertheless make racist remarks, [...] such statements would perhaps be acceptable in another context, but if you take a closer look and put them into context, they are racists or insult a religious community or homosexuals, for example."*

Post January 6th, social media platforms have tried to do more to crack down on hate speech and the dissemination of misinformation. Those who use social media in this context, however, often find the temporary bans they face as part of using the platform. The short suspension is not enough to curtail their rhetoric. The term "Facebook jail" is now used to describe the ban and is seen more of a joke than a punishment. The push to monitor content unfortunately has not stemmed the tide of hate crimes as we are still seeing high numbers of hate-based violence in the United States.

As stated earlier, social media and the internet are double-edged swords. While the information above has been about the dark, violent side of social media and the internet, there are many examples of the positives. Family and friends have reconnected, and people have found support groups for rare diseases from which they or a loved one may be suffering. If you ever need a stress reliever, there is not a shortage of baby animal videos you can watch. It's often harder to clean up a mess than to make it, and we currently are in the need to clean up the hate being propagated through social media.

A group called Unity Starts with U in Vancouver, created a grass-roots campaign against hate. They used their social media platforms to deliver positive messages to offset promoted hate. A study on the impact of this group showed a change in the perspective of the majority of respondents to the positive. The grassroots campaigns are increasing the initiative of the silent majority to speak out against bigotry and hate in the Vancouver area. The group is basically creating a virtual community to encourage people to speak out against hate. While this was done in only a small area, it shows the impact of a virtual community when it works against those who spread their hate.

After January 6th, there has been more work done to eliminate hate speech from social media. The reclaiming of social media will take the work of society and the government. Hate has become so ingrained in the platform many people ignore it, without the realization that hate can and does bleed into communities in the form of violence. While some claim it's a freedom granted by the Amendments of the Constitution, the First Amendment applies to governmental persecution of speech, not ramifications one may face from the private sector. The only way we can make headway against the rise in hate crimes is to push back against hate on the same platforms that allowed it to so easily spread.

Chapter 10 ~ Hope for the Future

Hope is a passion for the possible. —Soren Kierkegaard

This book has been a journey for me to complete. It started with a simple idea to use my story and that of my grandfather's to show how the spread of hate could be stopped. But as I mapped out the book and researched different areas of hate, it became more of a passion. I saw how hate can grow when supported by a society and how its impacts last long after the hate has ceased. The journey also helped me see how there is still so much work to be done to eradicate hate crimes and violence. It is easy to get discouraged when you read about attacks on people due to their heritage or religion. Even when positives occur, hate seems to overshadow them. Possibly because hate is so easily spread and was so before the advent of internet and social media. People who are insecure about their situation and role in society are infected with hate spread by others. While hate is infectious there has always been some who stand up against it. The continued violence against people makes it hard to determine if we are heading in the right direction as a society or if the virus of hate is spreading out of control.

Even before I started working on the book, certain news stories caught my eye. I would see a headline about attacks and violence against particular groups of people and felt compelled to read about what happened. It almost felt like I had to honor the victims by reading about the event. After starting the book, it seemed like I was seeing more articles about attacks. I would like to think it was because I was even more sensitive to headlines with certain words, but, unfortunately, hate crimes are on the rise. In terms of antisemitic attacks in the United States, there was a thirty-four percent increase in 2021 compared to 2020. The attacks ranged from swastikas painted on synagogues to physical attacks and shootings. 2022 did not see these attacks decrease, and 2023 has not shown any improvements.

As previously mentioned, anti-Asian hate saw an increase during the pandemic. While there was already contention about China and the loss of jobs overseas, the pandemic kicked hate into high gear. It did not matter if a person was of Chinese descent or from another Asia-Pacific country, they were targeted. While the hate crimes against people of Asian descent occurred early in the pandemic, it wasn't until an eighty-four-year-old Thai immigrant died after being punched by an assailant while on his walk that crimes against Asians were brought to the forefront of the news. Even beyond the violence, people of Asian descent have been targeted with verbal assaults as derogatory labels.

A friend of mine shared that her children, who were adopted from Asia, have been subjected to verbal insults due to their heritage. She didn't notice the insults until after pandemic lockdowns. America-born friends of Asian descent have experienced being told by others to go back to where they came from. For a nation made up of immigrants and descendants of immigrants, telling someone to go to where they came from goes against everything upon which this country was built. It also indicates how little it takes for a group to become a target of hate.

Since the beginning of recorded history genocide of varying degrees has occurred all over the world. Chinese government's treatment of Uyghurs population gained news coverage around the time I began writing this book. While working on the last few chapters, the Russian government invaded Ukraine. A planned visit to Lithuania as part of the book was abandoned as Ukraine hostilities and saber rattling against other NATO countries escalated. It's difficult to ignore Russia's treatment of Ukrainian people and deny genocide since Russian attacks seem to target Ukrainian civilians and cause total destruction of their cities.

For example, a key port and a center of trade and manufacturing, Mariupol, was bombed and reduced to rubble. It is now virtually unusable for trade or manufacturing. If the goal of the Russian government was conquest, one would think they'd have planned strategic attacks in terms of life and infrastructure losses. Instead, their strikes in Mariupol and elsewhere point to total Ukrainian citizen elimination. While a few Russian soldiers have been convicted of war crimes, Ukrainians, a people who Russians tried to eliminate a century ago, face daily continued violence.

Another way the Russian government is attempting to destroy the Ukrainians is by taking Ukrainian children into Russia to be adopted by Russian families. By doing this, the children will become indoctrinated into the Russian culture and lose their ties to Ukraine. If the children are young enough, they will maintain no memory of their families or their native culture. The International Criminal Court has issued an arrest warrant for the Russian President, Putin, but the damage is continuing to be done to the Ukrainian children who now find themselves adopted into Russian families.

As Russia continues their attacks on Ukraine, hate crimes occur in the United States, and laws are proposed and passed to disenfranchise the LBGTQ+ community, a better future can be built upon glimmers of hope. One glimmer was the convictions of people who killed Blacks. While the continued race-based killings ordinarily would not be seen as a sign of hope for the future, recent cases show a shift in public opinion. Part of the reason it's seen as a sign of hope is that just over thirty years ago, a video of an unarmed man, Rodney King, brutally beaten by LA police officers was shown on the news. Rodney King had been stopped after a high-speed chase and was being arrested for driving under the influence of drugs. In the civil trial that followed, the officers were found not guilty of the attack, even though the video showed the officers' illegal actions. While two were found guilty on federal charges, they were found not guilty in the civil state trial, which indicated society's view, in at least California, at the time.

In 2021, the trial of the officer charged with George Floyd's murder was held. After previous law officers had been acquitted for assaults against and murders of Blacks, some had little hope Floyd's trial would be any different. Unlike previous trials, the officer who kneeled on Floyd's neck for over nine minutes and the officers who did nothing to stop him were all found guilty by the state. The officer who was convicted of murder also pled guilty to federal charges of violating Floyd's civil rights.

When I heard the trial's verdict, I felt surprised the officer was convicted considering past officers had been set free, and I felt relief as it appeared times, in terms of race relations, were changing.

Another glimmer of hope was the conviction of three men who murdered Ahmaud Arbrey. Arbrey was jogging, when three men in their vehicles chased him down. When Arbrey tried to defend himself, the men shot and killed him. The father and son of the trio were sentenced to life in prison with no possibility of parole. The third man was sentenced to life in prison with the possibility of parole. Why that case offers hope is that the murder occurred in Georgia and three white men were convicted of killing a black man. Even sixty years ago, we might have seen a much different outcome. Granted, local officials attempted to dismiss the charges, but the Georgia government stepped in, and justice was served.

Social media has shown signs of combating hate. As the Unity Starts with U movement in Vancouver showed, flooding social media with positive messages reduced the amount of hate spread. Granted it was a small study, more like a drug trial, but it shows promise for what can happen with a concerted effort of people reclaiming social media. We cannot rely on social media companies to police the internet. As we have seen from instances, it took society as a whole working together to control hate speech.

In putting together this book, I spent much time researching past events. I felt that by understanding how hate grew and was supported, I might understand my grandfather more and also envisage a possible decline in hate crimes. The current movement to sanitize past atrocities to move forward is not the way to accomplish our goals.

German writer Siegfried Lenz stated, *"The past does not stop, it examines us in the present. It is this examination which we should all undergo, again and again. This way we preserve remembrance of the victims of the most perfidious crime against humanity and modern history. At the same time, this examination assists us in fighting racism, antisemitism, and anti-democratic behavior in the present. In this effort we must all unite, no matter which side of the abyss of history we occupy."*

It would be so simple to move forward without facing up to what we as humans have done to fellow humans. It also makes it easier to push any ancestorial guilt we may have into the dark recesses of our family closets. By facing up to what has been done, we deny the future potential for the kinds of hate and violence found in our pasts. It can be hard to learn about our ancestors' evil deeds.

A Dutch rescuer who studied the origination of the Nazi "monster" stated, *"I finally realized, every time you see the monster, you basically are looking in a mirror."*

The monster inside people is one those of us who've discovered these monsters in our family trees come to fear in ourselves. Perhaps that's why we work so hard to overcome the corruption of our ancestors through our own actions.

Browning, who examined the men in the German Reserve Battalion 101 involved in the Jews' extermination, put it best, *"If the men of Reserve Battalion 101 could become killers under such circumstances, which group of men cannot."*

In the tragedy of the Holocaust, there was an overlooked example of what happens when a society refuses to allow hate to dictate their actions. When Germany conquered Denmark, they attempted to recruit the Danish people to help them with the extermination of the Jewish people in Denmark. Instead of finding willing accomplices, they found a society that refused to help. Because the Danish people as a whole refused to assist the Nazis, the Danish Jews survived the war. So, while they lost their autonomy to govern themselves, they did not lose their moral compasses. If people in more countries would have done this, many more Jewish people would have survived the war. More importantly, it shows how when a people band together, they can stop what appears to be an unstoppable force of hate.

When I share with people my history and the belief my grandfather hiding his actions saved me from hate being passed on to me, some have said they believed I'd be the same person had he not hidden his crime. Even before researching, I had a hard time fully believing them. I imagined having open hate spewed in my presence every Sunday from the time I was born until I was in high school. I wondered if I would hold the beliefs I have today. Granted, I doubt my parents would've married if my mom grew up hearing similar hate, but, even so, I cannot in good conscience say I would not have bigoted views towards other people if my grandfather was free to speak his hate. Feeling like an outsider most of my life, what would have prevented me from using my loneliness to punish particular groups? Would I have used hate as a way of being part of a community and improving my self-esteem by trying to lower others? In this, I am grateful I did not hear hate speech when we visited my grandfather. I am grateful my grandfather isolated his hate from me. I hate the thought of not having the diversity of people that I have in my life. Fortunately, my circle sees the good in me and overlooks the evil in my family.

As I stated in my introduction, I was asked what I hoped to get from publishing my book. Whether my book helps others understand their relatives who may have committed atrocities or to find a way to come to terms with that knowledge, I do not know. I am not sure it will make an impact on how people stand up to hate in our world. I know my research has helped me understand my grandfather more and to come to better terms with the knowledge about him. It has helped me understand my mother better. It has also opened my eyes to how easy it is to have hate spread to a point of violence and how much work it takes to put an end to it and reverse the damage done.

I can hope maybe by sharing my research and story, others will stand against hate speech they see on social media and in public. As a society, I hope we quarantine hate and stop its spread. I know my book is not going to cause a sweeping change in the United States or the world, but maybe it can make a difference with one person somewhere. Maybe a person will know that how they feel about hate they've observed is mirrored by others. And, maybe instead of virtual hate communities, a community of inclusiveness and good can be created.

Afterword

Since completing the book and starting the publishing process, there have been disturbing trends in laws being suggested and passed in states. I feel like I would be remiss to not acknowledge this disturbing trend. These laws are mainly targeted towards the LBGTQ+ community, which is already highly marginalized. These laws are generally focused on the trans and drag segments of this community. The loud minority are pushing these laws because they want to "protect our children", which is a rallying cry that is often used to justify further marginalizing a minority group, from being sexualized and indoctrinated. These laws include the ability to ban books in libraries, to remove diversity offices in higher education institutions, and limit what can be taught in schools. The problem is that lawmakers in these states enacting these laws are emboldening people to take matters into their own hands. Target recently had their employees threatened with violence and displays destroyed because the store started carrying tuck bathing suits for adult trans women. These bathing suits would allow a segment of our society to feel comfortable going to the pool or the beach as they want to be. People say they do not understand why a person would not follow society's binary standard for gender and why a person does not feel like the gender marked on their birth certificate. One does not have to understand why they feel the way they do to know that as a society we cannot allow laws to be enacted that deny them the right to be who they are and to embolden those looking for a segment of our society to hate.

In terms of indoctrination, the definition of indoctrination is the process of teaching a person or group to accept a set of beliefs uncritically. By banning books, letting the minority determine what is appropriate for other people, and labeling certain segments of our society as a danger because they do not fit a certain mold of behavior, indoctrination is happening, but it is such that will cause the spread of hate. We are at a precipice of a critical moment in our society. It is up to what has been the silent majority to step up and change the course our society is setting off on if we ever want to see a society where those who hate are not allowed to spread their hatred. We need to quarantine the hate and stop the spread before it gets more out of hand.

Acknowledgements

This project would not have been completed without the help of several people who were there for me during the project itself and throughout periods of my life. When I was close to starting the project, I reached out to Ann-Gee who I knew had published books. We were both hired at the university at the same time and had been friends and colleagues for years. I sought out her publisher and the publishing process. What I got was a cheerleader who encouraged me to start the project and continue working toward finishing. She was also the first one to review many chapters and taught me volumes about writing methods. Our sessions also included trying good food I had never eaten before and fun watching our puppies play.

The hours I spent with Jeffrey going paragraph by paragraph were valuable, not only in helping with the book but also my writing skills. With how long it took for us to work through my first chapter, I thought it would take years to work through my book. His instruction on how to rewrite sentences allowed me to make edits and better write future chapters to speed up the review. His questions helped me find areas that needed more information and organize my thoughts. After all the time we spent together, it was bittersweet when we finished the last chapter. I was happy to be done with the review but knew I would miss the time we spent together working on the project.

I would not have been in the right mindset to do a project like this without the guidance and counsel from Rick. He pushed me to examine myself and my life events and helped me get a better perspective on the world and the people around me. I cannot thank him enough for all he has done for me.

Of course, I must acknowledge my family. I grew up in an environment free of hate towards others, the genesis of my worldview. They also encouraged me to take on challenges, which enabled me to take the leap to do this project. All I have accomplished so far in my life and all that is to come is because of them.

References

Introduction

Hate crime statistics. The United States Department of Justice. (2022, September 26). Retrieved October 5, 2022, from https://www.justice.gov/hatecrimes/hate-crime-statistics

Lah, K., & Kravarik, J. (2021, February 16). *Family of Thai immigrant, 84, says fatal attack 'was driven by hate'*. CNN. Retrieved October 6, 2022, from https://www.cnn.com/2021/02/16/us/san-francisco-vicharatanapakdee-asian-american-attacks/index.html

report, N.F.L. wire. (2021, March 10). *Patriots WR Julian Edelman writes open letter to Heat's Meyers Leonard*. NFL.com. Retrieved October 5, 2022, from https://www.nfl.com/news/patriots-wr-julian-edelman-writes-open-letter-to-heat-s-meyers-leonard

Chapter 1

Berg, M. (2011). *Popular Justice: A History of Lynching in America*. Ivan R. Dee.

Durso, R.M., & Jacobs, D. (2013). The Determinants of the Number of White Supremacist Groups: A Pooled Time-Series Analysis. *SOCIAL PROBLEMS, 60*(1), 128–144. https://doi.org/10.1525/sp.2013.10168

Jackson, P.I. (2019). Encouraging White Christian Nationalist Extremism in the United States and Europe by Ignoring Minority Protection. *Conference Papers —American Sociological Association*, 1–34.

Michener, W. (2012). The Individual Psychology of Group Hate. *Journal of Hate Studies*, 10(1), 15–48. https://doi.org/10.33972/jhs.112

Monroe, K.R. (2008). Cracking the Code of Genocide: The Moral Psychology of Rescuers, Bystanders, and Nazis during the Holocaust. *Political Psychology*, 29(5), 699–736.

Mulholland, S.E. (2010). Hate Fuel: On the Relationship Between Local Government Policy and Hate Group Activity. *Eastern Economic Journal, 36*(4), 480–499.

Naimark, N.M. (2016). *GENOCIDE: A World History*. Oxford University Press.

Perry, B., & Scrivens, R. (2018). A Climate for Hate? An Exploration of the Right-Wing Extremist Landscape in Canada. *Critical Criminology, 26*(2), 169–187. https://doi.org/10.1007/s10612-018-9394-y.

Rempel, J.K., Burris, C.T., & Fathi, D. (2019). Hate: Evidence for a motivational conceptualization. *Motivation & Emotion, 43*(1), 179–190. https://doi.org/10.1007/s11031-018-9714-2.

Staub, E. (2012). Doing Good, Doing Bad, Doing Nothing. *Zygon Journal, 47*(4), 821-842.

Walter, D.O. (1935). *Congressional Digest, 14*(6/7), 169–171.

Wiesen, S.J. (2018). American Lynching in the Nazi Imagination: Race and Extra-Legal Violence in 1930s Germany. *German History, 36*(1), 38–59. https://doi.org/10.1093/gerhis/ghx122

Zier, M. (2021). Crimes of Omission: State-Action Doctrine and Anti-Lynching Legislation in the Jim Crow Era. *Stanford Law Review*, 73(3), 777–819.

Chapter 5

Bubnys, A. (2019). "The Holocaust in Lithuania 1941–1944". In *The History of Jews in Lithuania*. Leiden, The Netherlands: Brill | Schöningh. doi: https://doi.org/10.30965/9783657705757_028

Vanagaitė R., & Zuroff, E. (2020). *Our people: Discovering Lithuania's hidden holocaust*. Rowman & Littlefield.

Chapter 6

Los Angeles Times. (2020, January 28). *Newly released photos suggest John Demjanjuk was Sobibor death camp guard*. Los Angeles Times. Retrieved October 6, 2022, from https://www.latimes.com/world-nation/story/2020-01-28/demjanjuk-sobibor-nazi-holocaust-death-camp

NPR. (2014, November 5). *How thousands of Nazis were 'rewarded' with life in the U.S.* NPR. Retrieved October 6, 2022, from https://www.npr.org/2014/11/05/361427276/how-thousands-of-nazis-were-rewarded-with-life-in-the-u-s

Chapter 7

Blood and Soil: Hate groups have always been around, but the clearly prejudiced attitude of U.S. President Donald Trump has encouraged some to come out into the open. (2018). *Canada & the World Backgrounder, 83*(3), 12–15.

Berg, M. (2011). *Popular Justice: A History of Lynching in America.* Ivan R. Dee.

Michener, W. (2012). The Individual Psychology of Group Hate. *Journal of Hate Studies, 10*(1), 15–48. https://doi.org/10.33972/jhs.112

Monroe, K.R. (2008). Cracking the Code of Genocide: The Moral Psychology of Rescuers, Bystanders, and Nazis during the Holocaust. *Political Psychology, 29*(5), 699–736.

Naimark, N.M. (2016). *GENOCIDE: A World History.* Oxford University Press.

Overy, R. (2014). "Ordinary Men," Extraordinary Circumstances: Historians, Social Psychology, and the Holocaust. *Journal of Social Issues, 70*(3), 515–530. https://doi.org/10.1111/josi.12075

Staub, E. (2012). Doing Good, Doing Bad, Doing Nothing. *Zygon Journal, 47*(4), 821-842.

Waller, J. (2001). Perpetrators of Genocide: An Explanatory Model of Extraordinary Human Evil. *Journal of Hate Studies, 1*(1), 5

Wiesen, S.J. (2018). American Lynching in the Nazi Imagination: Race and Extra-Legal Violence in 1930s Germany. *German History, 36*(1), 38–59. https://doi.org/10.1093/gerhis/ghx122

Chapter 8

Bezo, B., & Maggi, S. (2015). Living in "survival mode:" Intergenerational transmission of trauma from the Holodomor genocide of 1932–1933 in Ukraine. *Social Science & Medicine, 134*, 87–94. https://doi.org/10.1016/j.socscimed.2015.04.009

Bryant, D.T., Adams, T., Alejandre, A., & Gray, A.A. (2017). The Trauma Lens of Police Violence against Racial and Ethnic Minorities. *Journal of Social Issues, 73*(4), 852–871. https://doi.org/10.1111/josi.12251

Covington, C. (2018). A Tragic Inheritance: The Irresolvable Conflict for Children of Perpetrators. *British Journal of Psychotherapy, 34*(1), 114–131. https://doi.org/10.1111/bjp.12329

Durham, M., & Webb, S.S.N. (2014). Historical trauma: A panoramic perspective. *Brown University Child & Adolescent Behavior Letter, 30*(10), 1–6.

Hammel, A. (2019). 'I Believe That My Experience Began in the Womb and Was Later Absorbed through My Mother's Milk': Second Generation Trauma Narratives. *German Life and Letters, 72*(4), 556–569. https://doi.org/10.1111/glal.12249

Krysińska, K., & Lester, D. (2006). The Contribution of Psychology to the Study of the Holocaust. *Dialogue & Universalism, 16*(5/6), 141–156.

Mangassarian, S.L. (2016). 100 Years of Trauma: The Armenian Genocide and Intergenerational Cultural Trauma. *Journal of Aggression, Maltreatment & Trauma, 25*(4), 371–381. https://doi.org/10.1080/10926771.2015.1121191

Matz, D., Vogel, E.B., Mattar, S., & Montenegro, H. (2015). Interrupting Intergenerational Trauma: Children of Holocaust Survivors and the Third Reich. *Journal of Phenomenological Psychology, 46*(2), 185–205. https://doi.org/10.1163/15691624-12341295

Oxenberg, J. (2003). Mourning, Meaning, and Not Repeating: Themes of Dialogue Between Descendants of Holocaust Survivors and Descendants of Nazis. *Journal for the Psychoanalysis of Culture & Society, 8*(1), 77.

Parens, H. (2009). Aftermath of genocide – the fate of children of perpetrators. *International Journal of Applied Psychoanalytic Studies, 6*(1), 25–42. https://doi.org/10.1002/aps.187

Senfft, A. (2020). The Long Shadow of the Perpetrators. *European Judaism, 53*(2), 77–86. https://doi.org/10.3167/ej.2020.530208

Soyalp, N. (2020). Applying Transdisciplinarity: Exploring Transgenerational Traumas of Anatolia, Turkey. World Futures: *The Journal of General Evolution, 76*(8), 554–578. https://doi.org/10.1080/02604027.2020.1788358

Wieland, B.J. (2012). Holocaust victims and perpetrators. *Journal of Analytical Psychology, 57*(4), 413–424. https://doi.org/10.1111/j.1468-5922.2012.01983.x

Wilkins, E., Whiting, J., Watson, M., Russon, J., & Moncrief, A. (2013). Residual Effects of Slavery: What Clinicians Need to Know. *Contemporary Family Therapy: An International Journal, 35*(1), 14–28. https://doi.org/10.1007/s10591-012-9219-1

Chapter 9

Byman, D., & Joshi, A. (2020). Preventing the Next Social-media Genocide. *Survival (00396338) 62*(6), 125–152. https://doi.org/10.1080/00396338.2020.1851097

Costello, M., Long Cheng, Feng Luo, Hongxin Hu, Song Liao, Vishwamitra, N., Mingqi Li, & Okpala, E. (2021). COVID-19: A Pandemic of Anti-Asian Cyberhate. *Journal of Hate Studies, 17*(1), 108–118. https://doi.org/10.33972/jhs.198

Dave, A. (2021). #MassProtests: The Abjuring of the Other and Lessons from Gandhi. *Journal of Hate Studies, 17*(1), 52–63. https://doi.org/10.33972/jhs.202

Dimitroff, K. (2021). Mark Zuckerberg, Joe Manchin, and ISIS: What Facebook's International Terrorism Lawsuits Can Teach Us About the Future of Section 230 Reform. *Texas Law Review, 100*(1), 153–188.

Ellis, R.J. (2022). A Fairy Tale Gone Wrong: Social Media, Recursive Hate and the Politicization of Drag Queen Storytime. *Journal of Criminal Law, 86*(2), 94–108. https://doi.org/10.1177/00220183221086455

Ganesh, B. (2018). The Ungovernability of Digital Hate Culture. *Journal of International Affairs, 71*(2), 30–49.

Jakubowicz, A. (2017). Alt-right White Lite: trolling, hate speech and cyber racism on social media. *Cosmopolitan Civil Societies: An Interdisciplinary Journal, 9*(3), 41–60. https://doi.org/10.5130/ccs.v9i3.5655

Leung, C., & Frank, R. (2020). Unity Starts with U: A Case Study of a Counter-Hate Campaign Through the Use of Social Media Platforms. *Journal of Hate Studies, 16*(1), 69–83. https://doi.org/10.33972/jhs.146

Mixon, G. (2020). Not Your Father's Marketplace of Ideas: Hate Speech and the Fraudulent Marketplace of Ideas Created by Social Media. *Emory International Law Review*, 34(1), 399–433.

Munn, L. (2022). Sustainable Hate: How Gab Built a Durable "Platform for the People." *Canadian Journal of Communication, 47*(1), 219–240. https://doi.org/10.22230/cjc.2022v47n1a4037

Paasch-Colberg, S., & Strippel, C. (2021). "The Boundaries are Blurry horizontal ellipsis ": How Comment Moderators in Germany See and Respond to Hate Comments. *JOURNALISM STUDIES*. https://doi.org/10.1080/1461670X.2021.2017793

Chapter 10

A&E Television Networks. (2010, March 4). *LAPD officers beat Rodney King on camera*. History.com. Retrieved October 6, 2022, from https://www.history.com/this-day-in-history/police-brutality-caught-on-video

Brangham, W., & Wellford, R. (2022, April 29). *Antisemitic incidents hit a record high in 2021. what's behind the rise in Hate?* PBS. Retrieved October 6, 2022, from https://www.pbs.org/newshour/show/antisemitic-incidents-hit-a-record-high-in-2021-whats-behind-the-rise-in-hate

Chappell, B. (2021, June 25). *Derek Chauvin is sentenced to 22 1/2 years for George Floyd's murder.* NPR. Retrieved October 6, 2022, from https://www.npr.org/sections/trial-over-killing-of-george-floyd/2021/06/25/1009524284/derek-chauvin-sentencing-george-floyd-murder

Lah, K., & Kravarik, J. (2021, February 16). *Family of Thai immigrant, 84, says fatal attack 'was driven by hate'.* CNN. Retrieved October 6, 2022, from https://www.cnn.com/2021/02/16/us/san-francisco-vicha-ratanapakdee-asian-american-attacks/index.html

Leung, C., & Frank, R. (2020). Unity Starts with U: A Case Study of a Counter-Hate Campaign Through the Use of Social Media Platforms. *Journal of Hate Studies, 16*(1), 69–83. https://doi.org/10.33972/jhs.146

Monroe, K. R. (2008). Cracking the Code of Genocide: The Moral Psychology of Rescuers, Bystanders, and Nazis during the Holocaust. *Political Psychology, 29*(5), 699–736.

Yancey-Bragg, N., & Habersham, R. (2022, August 9). *Georgia dad, son sentenced to life for hate crimes in Ahmaud Arbery death; 3rd defendant gets 35 years.* USA Today. Retrieved October 6, 2022, from https://www.usatoday.com/story/news/nation/2022/08/08/ahmaud-arbery-federal-hate-crime-sentencing/10263789002/

www.ingramcontent.com/pod-product-compliance
Lightning Source LLC
Chambersburg PA
CBHW062115080426

42734CB00012B/2875